EDITION FREIZEIT UND WISSEN
UNTERWASSERFÜHRER BAND 8
Herausgeber: Dr. Friedrich Naglschmid

Unterwasserführer

Madeira - Kanaren - Azoren

Fische

Underwater Guide

Madeira - Canary Islands - Azores

Fish

Dr. Peter Wirtz

VERLAG STEPHANIE NAGLSCHMID STUTTGART

Die Deutsche Bibliothek - CIP-Einheitsaufnahme

Unterwasserführer Madeira - Kanaren - Azoren: Fische =
Underwater Guide Madeira - Canary Islands - Azores: Fish /
Peter Wirtz. - Stuttgart : Naglschmid, 1994
    (Edition Freizeit und Wissen : Unterwasserführer ; Band 8)
    ISBN 3-927913-29-4
NE: Wirtz, Peter; Underwater Guide Madeira - Canary Islands - Azores:
Fish; Edition Freizeit und Wissen / Unterwasserführer

Fotos: Einzelnachweise S. 158
Titelfoto: Dr. Peter Wirtz / MTi-Press
Titelgestaltung: Dr. Friedrich Naglschmid / MTi-Press
Foto Umschlagrückseite: Dr. Beate Müller / MTi-Press
Zeichnungen: Stephanie Naglschmid / MTi-Press
Lektorat: Helmut Göthel / MTi-Press
Engl. Übersetzung: John Broad / MTi-Press und Dr. Peter Wirtz / MTi-Press

Alle in diesem Buch enthaltenen Angaben, Daten, Ergebnisse usw. wurden von dem Autor nach bestem Wissen erstellt und von ihm und vom Verlag sorgfältig überprüft. Gleichwohl können inhaltliche Fehler nicht vollständig ausgeschlossen werden. Daher erfolgen die gemachten Angaben, Daten, Ergebnisse usw. ohne jegliche Verpflichtung oder Garantie des Autors oder des Verlags. Weder der Autor noch der Verlag übernehmen irgendeine Verantwortung und Haftung für etwaige inhaltliche Unrichtigkeiten.

Geschützte Warennamen und Warenzeichen werden nicht besonders gekennzeichnet. Aus dem Fehlen solcher Hinweise kann nicht geschlossen werden, daß es sich um freie Warennamen bzw. freie Warenzeichen handelt.

Alle Rechte, insbesondere das Recht der Vervielfältigung und Verbreitung und der Übersetzung, vorbehalten. Kein Teil des Werkes darf in irgendeiner Form (durch Fotokopie, Mikrofilm oder ein anderes Verfahren) ohne schriftliche Genehmigung des Verlages reproduziert werden oder unter Verwendung elektronischer Systeme verarbeitet, vervielfältigt oder verbreitet werden.

COPYRIGHT 1994 VERLAG STEPHANIE NAGLSCHMID
Rotebühlstr. 87 A, 70178 Stuttgart
Tel. 0711/626878, Fax 0711/612323

Unsere Bücher werden auf chlorfrei gebleichtem Papier gedruckt.

Herstellung: Druckerei Schreck GmbH u. Co. KG, 67487 Maikammer/Pfalz

INHALT - CONTENTS

Inhaltsverzeichnis - Contents   3
Einleitung - Preface   8
Schema eines Knochenfisches - Scheme of a bone fish   15
Gebrauchsanleitung - How to use this book   16

Teufelsrochen - Devil Rays   18

Adlerrochen - Eagle Rays   20

Stechrochen - Stingrays   22

Schmetterlingsrochen - Butterfly Rays   24

Zitterrochen - Electric Rays   24

Echte Rochen - Skates   26

Eidechsenfische - Lizardfish   28

Muränen - Moray Eels   30

Zauberaale - Sorcerer Eels   36

Schlangenaale - Snake Eels   36

Meerale - Conger Eels	38
Halbschnäbler - Halfbeaks	42
Hornhechte - Needlefish	42
Dorsche - Codfish	44
Ährenfische - Sand Smelts	46
Trompetenfische - Trumpetfish	46
Seenadeln und Seepferdchen - Pipefish and Seahorses	48
Schnepfenfische - Snipefish	50
Heringe - Herrings	50
Barrakudas - Barracudas	52
Meeräschen - Mullets	52
Eberfische - Boarfish	54
Heringskönige - Dories	54

Zackenbarsche - Groupers	56
Kardinalbarsche - Cardinalfish	62
Großaugenbarsche - Bigeyes	64
Meerbrassen - Breams	66
Pilotbarsche - Sea Chubs	78
Meerbarben - Goatfish	78
Grunzer - Grunts	80
Blaubarsche - Bluefish	82
Stachelmakrelen - Jacks	84
Riffbarsche - Damselfish	90
Lippfische - Wrasses	94
Papageifische - Parrotfish	106
Petermännchen - Weevers	108

Himmelsgucker - Stargazers   110

Schiffshalter - Sharksuckers   110

Makrelen und Tune - Mackerels and Tunas   112

Dreiflosser - Triplefin Blennies   114

Blenniiden - Blennies   116

Beschuppte Blenniiden - Scaled Blennies   122

Grundeln - Gobies   124

Knurrhähne - Gurnards   126

Skorpionsfische - Scorpionfish   128

Butte - Left-eye Flounders   130

Seezungen - Soles   132

Hundszungen - Tonguesoles   132

Drückerfische - Triggerfish   134

Feilenfische - Filefish	134
Kugelfische - Pufferfish	136
Igelfische - Porcupine Fish	138
Ansauger - Clingfish	140
Eingeweidefische - Pearlfish	142
Krötenfische - Frogfishes	144

Namen der Arten auf Madeira, den Azoren und den Kanaren - Madeiran, Azorean and Canarian names of the species	146
Index Deutsch - Index German	149
Index Englisch - Index English	152
Index Latein - Index Latin	155
Bildnachweis - Photo Credit	158
Literaturverzeichnis - Bibliography	158
Danksagung - Acknowledgement	159

Die glückseligen Inseln

Die "Makaronesischen Inseln" liegen nicht etwa irgendwo im Südpazifik, wie man nach dem Namen vermuten könnte. Der deutsche Botaniker A. Engler prägte 1879 diesen Begriff für die Azoren, Madeira (plus Porto Santo) und die Kanaren, und zwar aufgrund von Ähnlichkeiten in der Pflanzenwelt dieser Inseln. Der Name kommt aus dem Griechischen (makaros, nesios) und bedeutet "die glückseligen Inseln". Später wurden von vielen Autoren oft auch noch die Kapverdischen Inseln zu den Makaronesen gezählt, aber neue Untersuchungen haben gezeigt, daß die Kapverden eine viel größere Ähnlichkeit zum tropischen Afrika haben als zu den Makaronesischen Inseln. Auch wenn wir uns als Beispiel eine kleine Fischgruppe, die Blennies (Seite 114-123) anschauen, zeigt sich dieses Muster (siehe Abbildung Seite 13): 80% der Arten von Madeira und den Azoren sind gleich und 67% der Arten von Madeira und den Kanaren, aber die Ähnlichkeit im Artbestand zu den Kapverden ist viel geringer. Elf Fischarten leben nur bei Madeira, den Kanaren und den Azoren und nirgendwo sonst; eine davon ist der Makaronesen-Zackenbarsch (Seite 56).

Mit 1.500 km Entfernung zum Festland sind die Azoren die abgelegenste Inselgruppe im nördlichen Atlantik (siehe Tabelle Seite 12). Eine Folge dieser isolierten Lage ist, daß es nur etwa 400 Fischarten bei den Azoren gibt (je etwa 550 bei Madeira und bei den Kanaren): manche Küstenfische haben den Sprung über den weiten Ozean nicht geschafft. Ein Beispiel ist die artenreiche Familie der Meerbrassen (Seite 66-77): während es bei den Kanaren 24 verschiedene Arten gibt und 15 bei Madeira, sind nur 7 Meerbrassen Arten von den Azoren bekannt.

Die Angaben über die Verbreitung der Fischarten in diesem Buch beruhen auf dem neuesten Stand des Wissens. Für die Kanarischen Inseln ist gerade ein Katalog aller von dort bekannten Fische erschienen und zusammen mit Wissenschaftlern von den Azoren und von Madeira arbeitet der Autor gerade an entsprechenden Katalogen für diese beiden Gebiete. In diesem Buch ist die Verbreitung der Arten mit "M, K, A" für "Madeira, Kanaren, Azoren" angegeben. Wenn Sie womöglich eine Art an einer Inselgruppe fotografiert haben, bei der diese Art noch gar nicht registriert ist, so schicken Sie doch bitte einen Papierabzug des Fotos an die jeweilige Meldezentrale, nämlich:

Madeira: Dr. M. Biscoito
Museu Municipal
P - 9000 Funchal, Madeira, Portugal
Kanaren: Dr. A. Brito
Dept. Biologia Animal
Universidade de la Laguna
E - 38206 La Laguna, Tenerife, Islas Canarias

Azoren: Dr. R. S. Santos
Dept. Oceanografia e Pescas
Universidade dos Azores
P - 9900 Horta, Faial, Açores, Portugal

Mit Ausnahme der beiden Kanareninseln Fuerteventura und Lanzarote, die als Abspaltungen vom Afrikanischen Festland entstanden sind, sind alle Inseln vulkanischen Ursprungs. Aus zum Teil mehreren tausend Metern Tiefe kommend ragen diese riesigen Vulkane nur mit ihren Spitzen aus dem Wasser. Im gleichen Meeresgebiet gibt es noch viele andere Vulkane, die die Meeresoberfläche nicht erreichen; manche davon waren aber wahrscheinlich in früheren Zeiten, als der Meersspiegel mindestens 100 m tiefer lag, ebenfalls Inseln auf denen Landpflanzen und Landtiere lebten.

Die gebirgige Landschaft im Landesinneren lädt zu Spaziergängen und Bergwanderungen ein und führt immer wieder zu großartigen Ausblicken wie etwa den auf den Adlerfelsen von Madeira (Abbildung Seite 17). Madeira, die Kanaren und die Azoren sind deshalb auch für nicht-tauchende Familienmitglieder ideale Urlaubsziele und eben für Taucher, die sich sowohl über als auch unter Wasser von einer reizvollen Mischung aus Europa und Afrika bezaubern lassen wollen, den glückseligen Inseln.

The Blissful Islands

The "Macaronesian Islands" are not, as the name appears to indicate, somewhere in the South Pacific. The German botanist A. Engler gave this name to the Azores, Madeira (plus Porto Santo) and the Canaries in 1879, because of similarities in the plant life of these islands. The name comes from the Greek (makaros, nesios) and means "the blissful islands". Later on, many authors also included the Cape Verde Islands into the Macaronesian islands, but new research has shown that the Cape Verde Islands are more similar to tropical mainland Africa than to the Macaronesian islands. If we take as an example a small fish group, the Blennies (page 114-123), we see the same pattern (see figure page 13): 80% of the species of Madeira and the Azores are the same and 67% of the species of Madeira and the Canaries are the same, whereas the degrees of similarity to the Cape Verde Islands are much lower. Eleven fish species live only at Madeira, the Canaries and the Azores and nowhere else; one of them is the Comb Grouper (page 56).

With a distance of 1.500 km to the continent, the Azores are the remotest group of islands in the northern Atlantic (see table page 12). It is due to this isolated position, that only about 400 fish species exist at the Azores (whereas at Madeira and at the Canaries there exist about 550): many coastal fish were not able to cross the wide ocean. An example is the family of the Breams (page 66-77) which has many species: whereas at the Canaries there exist 24 different species, and 15 at Madeira, only 7 species of Breams are known to exist at the Azores.

The information on the distribution of species of fish in this book is based on the latest state of knowledge. For the Canary islands, a catalogue of all the fishes known to exist there has just been printed and I am currently working, together with scientists from Madeira and the Azores, on the same kind of catalogue for both these areas. In this book, the distribution of the species is indicated by the letters "M, K, A" for "Madeira, Canaries, Azores" respectivly. If you possibly have a photograph of a species from one of the island groups, where the species has not yet been registred, then please send a paper copy of the photo to the respective information centre, namely:

Madeira: Dr. M. Biscoito
               Museu Municipal
               P - 9000 Funchal, Madeira, Portugal
Canaries: Dr. A. Brito
               Dept. Biologia Animal
               Universidade de la Laguna
               E - 38206 La Laguna, Tenerife, Islas Canarias

Azores: Dr. R. S. Santos
Dept. Oceanografia e Pescas
Universidade dos Acores
P - 9900 Horta, Faial, Açores, Portugal

With the exeption of the two Canary islands Fuerteventura and Lanzarote, which originated by splitting off from the African mainland, all the islands have a volcanic origin. Coming from depths of several thousand meters, these gigantic volcanoes jut out of the water only with their tips. In the same sea area there are many more volcanoes which do not break above the surface; some of these probably were islands in former times, when the water level was at least 100 m deeper, islands on which lived land plants and land animals.

The mountanous landscape of the central regions of the islands invite one to take walks and to go on mountain tours which ever again lead to magnificent views such as the one from the Eagles' Rock at Madeira (picture on page 17). Therefore, Madeira, the Canaries and the Azores are ideal spots for holidays, also for non-diving family members and especially for divers, who want to let themselves be enchanted by a charming mixture of Europe and Africa not only above but also under water, the Blissful Islands.

	Anzahl Inseln	Fläche (km²)	höchste Erhebung (m)	Entfernung zum Festland (km)
Azoren	9	2304	2351	1450
Madeira	2 (+4)	796	1861	610
Kanaren	7 (+3)	7273	3708	100

Tabelle: Geograpische Daten von den Azoren, Madeira und den Kanaren im Vergleich

	number of islands	surface area (km²)	highest mountain (m)	distance to mainland (km)
Azores	9	2304	2351	1450
Madeira	2 (+4)	796	1861	610
Canary Islands	7 (+3)	7273	3708	100

table: Geographic parameters of the Azores, Madeira and the Canary Islands in comparison

Abbildung rechte Seite: Ähnlichkeit des Artbestandes der Makaronesischen Inseln am Beispiel der Blennies.
figure right side: Degrees of similarity in species from the Macaronesian Islands, the example of blennies.

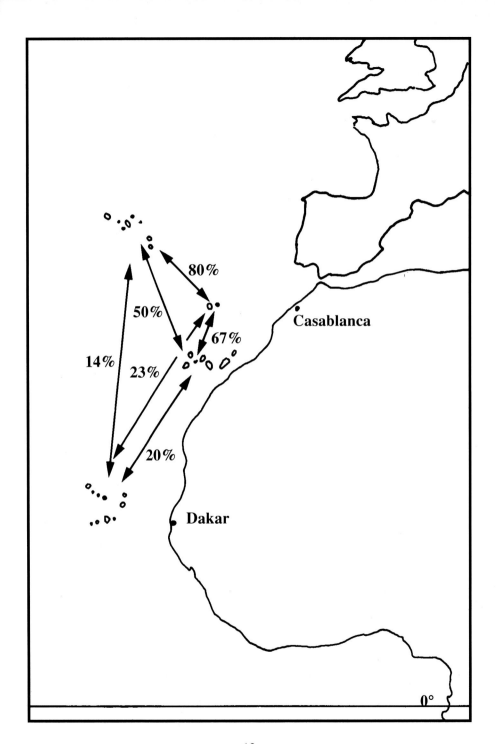

Gebrauchsanleitung

Erläuerung des Piktogramms

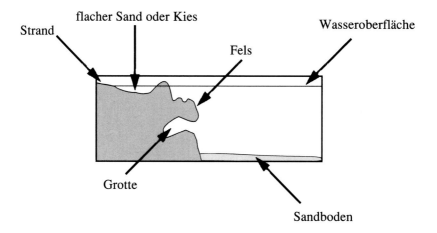

Im Piktogramm weisen ein oder mehrere kleine schwarze Pfeile auf den oder die bevorzugten Standorte der vorgestellten Fischart hin.

tag-　　　　dämmerungs-　　　　nachtaktiv

3	Ein (am oberen Ende und an der Spitze mit einer Meterangabe versehener) senkrechter Pfeil gibt an, in welchem Tiefenbereich sich die Fische bevorzugt aufhalten.
>30	Ein an der Pfeilspitze gesetztes >30 weist darauf hin, daß die beschriebene Fischart auch noch in größerer Tiefe als der empfohlenen maximalen Tauchtiefe von 30 m vorkommt.

How to use this Book

Explanation of the diagram

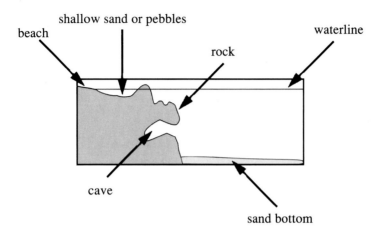

A single or several black arrows in the diagramm indicate the preferred habitats of the species depicted.

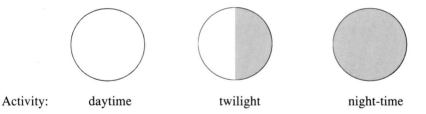

Activity: daytime   twilight   night-time

3
>30

A vertical arrow with numbers at the top and at the point indicates the range of the depth (in metres) within which the fish are normaly found. The figure >30 at the tip of the arrow indicates that this species can also be found below the maximum diving depth of 30 metres recommended.

SCHEMA EINES KNOCHENFISCHES
SCHEME OF A BONY FISH

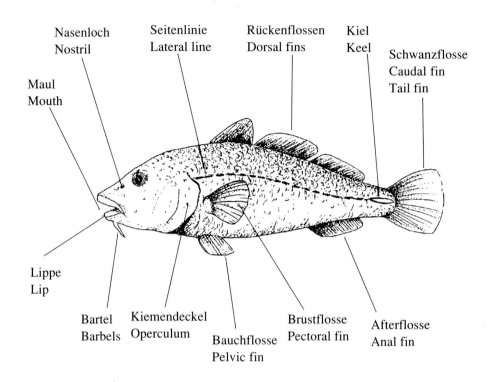

Adlerfelsen von Madeira

Agulo auf Gomera

Eagles' Rock at Madeira

Agulo on Gomera

Teufelsrochen   Devil Rays   Mobulidae
Manta   Manta ray   Manta birostris

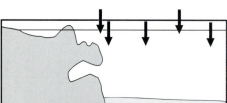
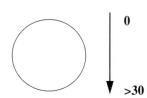

Teufelsrochen sind große, frei schwimmende Rochen, die sich von Plankton ernähren. Die Kopflappen dienen wahrscheinlich dazu, das Wasser in den Mund zu leiten. Plankton (und kleine Fische) werden mit einem Reusenapparat an den Kiemen ausgesiebt. Die Kopflappen können auch eingerollt werden (unteres Bild) und ragen dann wie Hörner nach vorne, was den Tieren den Namen gegeben hat. Teufelsrochen tragen oft Schiffshalter (siehe Seite 21 und Seite 110). M.

Devil rays are large, free-swimming rays which feed on plankton. Their head-flaps are probably used to guide the water into the mouth. Plankton (along with small fish) are sieved through the gills with the aid of a sieving apparatus. The head-flaps can also be rolled up (bottom picture) and projected forth resembling horns, which gave the animals their name. Devil rays often transport sharksuckers (see page 21 and page 110). M.

Teufelsrochen   Devil Rays   Mobulidae

Kleiner Teufelsrochen   **Small devil ray**   **Mobula mobular**

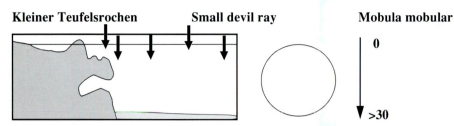

Im Gegensatz zum Manta (bis zu 7 m Flügelspannweite) kommt der Kleine Teufelsrochen auf "nur" max. 5 m Spannweite. Er hat viel kürzere Kopflappen und eine weiter hinten unten liegende Mundöffnung. Die Körperoberseite ist eher grünlich (bräunlich bis schwarz beim Manta). Das Tier auf dem Foto hat seine Kopflappen eingerollt; an seiner Bauchseite hängt ein Schiffshalter (Seite 104). M, K, A.

Contrary to the manta ray (wingspan up to 7 m) the small devil ray's wingspan reaches "only" a maximum of 5 m. Its head-flaps are much shorter, and its mouth opening is much further to the back and further down than the manta`s. The topside of its body is a green hue (brown to black in the manta ray). The animal in the photo has its head-flaps rolled up; a sharksucker (page 104) is attached to its belly. M, K, A.

Adlerrochen   Eagle Rays   Myliobatidae

Adlerrochen   **Eagle ray**   **Myliobatis aquila**

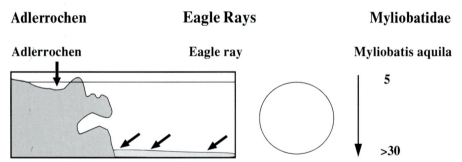

Wie die Stechrochen (Seite 22-25) haben auch die Adlerrochen ein oder zwei Giftstacheln auf dem Schwanz. Bei Adlerrochen ist der Schwanz sehr lang und dünn. Am Ansatz des Schwanzes, dicht vor den Stacheln, steht eine kleine Rückenflosse (bei Stechrochen fehlt sie). Adlerrochen graben in Sand und Schlammboden nach Muscheln, die sie mit ihren kräftigen Pflasterzähnen zermalmen. Wahrscheinlich können sie die im Boden vergrabenen Muscheln riechen. M, K, A.

Similar to the stingrays (page 22), eagle rays also have one or two poisoned spines on their tails. The eagle ray's tail is very long and thin. In the beginning of the tail, just before the spine, is a small dorsal fin (which does not exist in stingrays, page 22-25). Eagle rays dig in sand or mud for shellfish, which they then crush in their powerful plaster-stone like teeth. They can probably smell out the shellfish which are buried in the sand. M, K, A.

| Kleiner Teufelsrochen | Small devil ray | Mobula mobular |
| Adlerrochen | Eagle ray | Myliobatis aquila |

Stechrochen	Stingrays	Dasyatidae
Schwarzer Stechrochen Brauner Stechrochen	Round stingray Common stingray	Taeniura grabata Dasyatis pastinaca

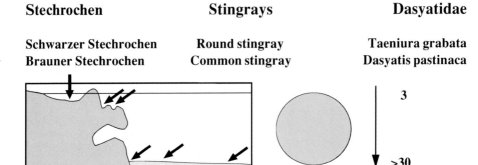

Stechrochen tragen ein bis zwei Giftstacheln auf dem Schwanz. Die Zahl ist variabel, weil die Stacheln regelmäßig abgeworfen und gewechselt werden. Eine Rückenflosse haben Stechrochen im Gegensatz zu Adlerrochen (Seite 20) nicht. Der Giftstachel besteht aus einer dem Zahnschmelz ähnlichen Substanz. Er trägt Widerhaken (kleines Bild) und ist beim lebenden Tier von einer Giftdrüse umgeben. Stechrochen setzen ihre Waffen ausschließlich zur Verteidigung ein, allerdings auch gegen Taucher, die ihnen zu dicht auf den Leib rücken. Ähnlich wie ein Skorpion schlägt der sich bedroht fühlende Rochen seitlich oder über den Kopf mit seinem Schwanz nach dem Angreifer.
Der Braune Stechrochen ist an seiner auffallend spitzen Schnauze und dem langen Schwanz zu erkennen. Der Schwarze Stechrochen hat einen viel kürzeren Schwanz und einen rundlichen Körperumriß. Beide hier abgebildeten Arten können Spannweiten von über 1,5 m und Längen bis zu 2,5 m erreichen.
Beide Arten M, K, A.

Stingrays have either one or two poisoned spines on their tails. The number is variable, as the spikes are regularly dropped and replaced. Contrary to eagle rays (page 20), sting rays do not have a dorsal fin. The spine is similar, in substance, to an enamel tooth. It has barbed hooks (small photo) and when on a live animal, is surrounded by a poison gland. Stingrays use these weapons of theirs exclusively for defence against anything, including divers, which approaches them too closely. Similar to a scorpion, a sting ray feeling threatened strikes out flinging its tail either to its side or over its head towards its attacker.
The Coomon sting ray can be recognized by its remarkably pointed snout and its long tail. The Round stingray has a much shorter tail and a roundish body contour. Both these species can have a wingspan of over 1,5 m and can reach 2,5 m in length.
Both species M, K, A.

| Schwarzer Stechrochen | Round stingray | Taeniura grabata |
| Brauner Stechrochen | Common stingray | Dasyatis pastinaca |

Schmetterlingsrochen   Butterfly Rays   Gymnuridae

Schmetterlingsrochen   Butterfly ray   Gymnura altavela

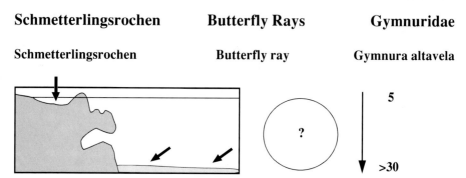

Die Brustflossen der Schmetterlingsrochen sind ganz besonders lang. Schmetterlingsrochen gehören auch in die Unterordnung der Stechrochenähnlichen und haben zwei Stacheln an ihrem besonders kurzen Schwanz. Sie erreichen Spannweiten von über 2 m, meistens sieht man aber Tiere mit etwa 1m Spannweite. M, K.

The pectoral fins of the butterfly rays are particularly long. Butterfly rays also belong to the suborder of the stingray-relatives and have two spines on their notably short tails. They can reach a wingspan of over 2 m although most animals seen have a wingspan of about 1m. M, K,

Zitterrochen   Electic Rays   Torpedinidae

Gefleckter Zitterrochen   Marbled electic ray   Torpedo marmorata

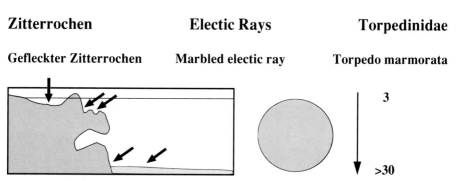

Um ihre Beute (kleine Fische und Krebse) zu betäuben und um sich zu verteidigen, können Zitterrochen Stromstöße von bis zu 220 V abgeben. Jeder Stromstoß besteht in Wirklichkeit aus einer Serie von 3-5 Stromschlägen, die jeweils weniger als eine hundertstel Sekunde dauern. Tagsüber sind die Tiere meistens im Sand vergraben. Typisch für Zitterrochen ist die fast kreisrunde Körperscheibe und der Besitz von zwei kleinen Rückenflossen auf dem kurzen Schwanz. M, K.

To stun their prey or to defend themselves, electric rays can emit an electric current of up to 220 V. Each discharge does in fact consist of a series of 3-5 discharges, each one lasting less than a hundreth of a second. During the day these animals are normally buried in the sand. The round disc-shaped bodies and the position of the two small dorsal fins on thei short tails is typical of electric rays. M, K.

| Schmetterlingsrochen | Butterfly ray | Gymnura altavela |
| Gefleckter Zitterrochen | Marbled electic ray | Torpedo marmorata |

25

Echte Rochen   Skates   Rajidae

Nagelrochen   Thornback ray   Raja clavata
Marmorrochen   Undulate ray   Raja undulata

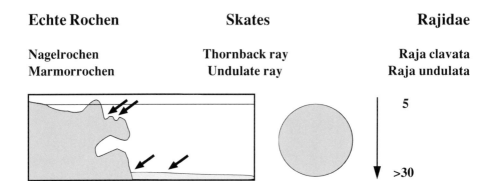

Während alle bisher besprochenen Arten von Rochen lebendgebärend sind, legen die Echten Rochen Eier, die mit einer vierzipfeligen, festen, schwarzen oder braunen Kapsel umhüllt sind. Die Embryonen brauchen mehrere Monate Entwicklungszeit. Leere Eikapseln werden manchmal am Strand angespült; auf englisch heißen sie "Geldbörsen von Seejungfrauen" (meermaids' purses).
Der Nagelrochen hat ein riesiges Verbreitungsgebiet, von Island im Norden, im Mittelmeer und Schwarzen Meer, bis zur Südspitze Afrikas und in den Indischen Ozean (also auch M, K, A). Er wird bis etwa 1m lang.
Ob es den Marmorrochen wirklich bei den Kanarischen Inseln gibt, oder ob diese Angabe auf einer Falschmeldung beruht, ist noch umstritten (Fotonachweise werden gesucht: siehe Einleitung); das Foto stammt von der Algarve. K?

Whilst all aforementioned species of rays are live-bearers, skates lay eggs, which are enveloped in a four-tipped, tight, black or brown capsule. The embryos need many months to evolve. Empty egg-cases are sometimes thrown onto the beach; in English they are called "Mermaids` purses". The thornback ray has an enormous distribution area, from Iceland in the north, in the Black Sea and Meditteranean, to the southern tip of Africa and in the Indian ocean (therefore also M, K, A.). It can reach a length of 1 m.
Whether the Undulate ray really exists in the Canaries or whether this information is false, is as of yet uncertain. (Photo evidence is required: see introduction); this photo was taken in the Algarve. K?

| Nagelrochen | Thornback ray | Raja clavata |
| Marmorrochen | Undulate ray | Raja undulata |

Eidechsenfische   Lizardfish   Synodontidae

Grüner Eidechsenfisch   Green lizardfish   Synodus saurus

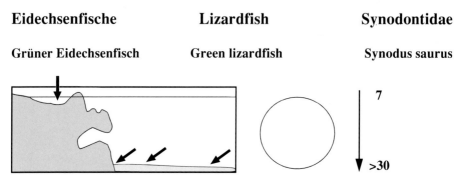

Eidechsenfische sind lauernde Raubfische. Mit ihren riesigen Mäulern können sie auch größere Fische schnappen, die zu dicht an ihnen vorbeischwimmen.
Der Grüne Eidechsenfisch lebt vor allem auf Sand- und Schlammboden. Gelegentlich kommt er auch auf Schotterboden vor; dort überlappen sich dann die Umweltansprüche der beiden Eidechsenfischarten, und manchmal kann man beide Arten nebeneinander sehen. M, K, A.

Lizardfish are lurking predators. They can catch even fairly large fish passing close to their enourmous mouths.
The green lizardfish lives mostly on sand and mud covered sea-beds. Occasionally it can be found on gravel. There the habitat requirements of the two species of lizardfish overlap and sometimes both species can be seen close to each other. M, K, A.

Brauner Eidechsenfisch   Brown lizardfish   Synodus synodus

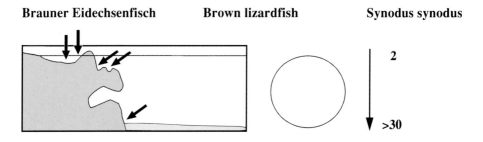

Der Braune Eidechsenfisch hat nicht immer so deutliche braune Querbänder wie auf dem Foto, aber der schwarze Fleck an der Basis der Brustflosse ist immer zu sehen. Er kommt auf vor allem auf Fels- und Geröllboden vor, selten auch auf Sandboden. M, K, A.

The brown lizardfish does not always have such distinct brown diagonal stripes as the animal in the photo, but the black spot on the base of the pectoral fin is always present. This fish can be found on a rocky or a pebble covered sea-bed but seldom on a sandy bottom. M, K, A.

| Grüner Eidechsenfisch | Green lizardfish | Synodus saurus |
| Brauner Eidechsenfisch | Brown lizardfish | Synodus synodus |

Muränen	Moray Eels	Muraenidae
Schwarze Muräne	Black moray	*Muraena augusti*

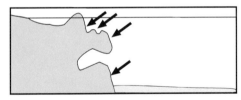 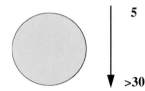

Im Gegensatz zu den Meeraalen (Seite 36) haben Muränen keine Brustflossen. Die meisten Arten sind nachtaktiv und liegen tagsüber ruhig in Höhlen und Spalten: geduldige und in der Regel völlig harmlose Fotomotive. Gefährlich sind nur angefütterte Muränen, die vom Taucher Futter erwarten und schon auch mal (versehentlich) nach Händen schnappen.
Die Schwarze Muräne wurde lange für eine Farbvariante der Mittelmeer-Muräne (Seite 32) gehalten, unterscheidet sich aber nicht nur in der Färbung (besonders auffallend: die weißen Augen) sondern auch in der Kopfform: die Schnauze ist etwas länger als bei der Mittelmeer-Muräne. M, K, A.

Contrary to the conger eels (page 38) moray eels have no pectoral fins. Most species are night-active and lie quietly in holes and cracks during the day. They are normally indulgent and totally harmless photo models.
Morays regularly being fed, however, can be dangerous, as those which are expecting to be fed can, mistakenly, snap at the hand of the diver. For a long time, black morays were considered just a colour variety of the mediteranean moray (page 32), but they not only differ in colour (especially the very striking white eyes) but also in the shape of their head. The snout is somewhat longer than that of the mediteranean morays. M, K, A.

Schwarze Muräne   Black moray   *Muraena augusti* ▶

Muränen Moray Eels Muraenidae

Mittelmeer-Muräne **Mediterranean moray** **Muraena helena**

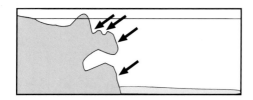 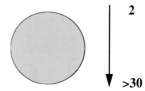

2
>30

Muränen haben keine Giftzähne, aber ihr Körperschleim und ihr Blut können zu Entzündungen führen, wenn sie in offene Wunden geraten. Bei der Jagd orientieren sich die meisten Muränen geruchlich. Deshalb haben viele Arten röhrenähnlich verlängerte Nasenöffnungen. Das blitzschnelle Zubeißen wird durch Berührungskontakt der Nahrung mit hochempfindlichen Zellen auf den Lippen und im gesamten Kopfbereich ausgelöst. Die Schleimhülle schlafender Papageifische (siehe Seite 106) ist anscheinend "chemisch neutral" und löst bei Berührung keinen Biß aus; sie dient zum Schutz vor jagenden Muränen. M, K, A.
Sowohl die Mittelmeer-Muräne als auch die Schwarze Muräne (Seite 30) werden bis 1,5 m lang.

Although morays do not have poison teeth, their body slime and their blood can lead to infection, if they enter an open wound. To hunt, most morays orientat by their sense of smell. It is due to this that many species have prolonged tube-like nostrils. The lightning-quick bite comes after contact of the food with extremly sensitive cells on the lips and in the whole region of the head. The slime envelope of sleeping Parrot fish (see page 106) appears to be "chemically neutral" and when touched does not elicit a bite; its protects against hunting morays. M, K, A.
Not only the mediteranean moray, but also the black moray grows to a length of 1,5 m.

Mittelmeer-Muräne Mediterranean moray Muraena helena ▶

Muränen   Moray Eels   Muraenidae

Maskenmuräne   Brown moray   Gymnothorax unicolor

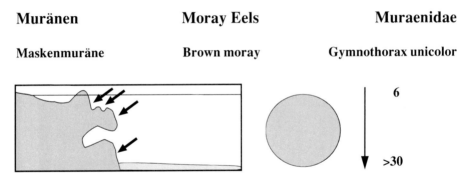

An ihrer kurzen bulldoggen-ähnlichen Schnauze und der dunklen "Bankräubermaske" ist die Maskenmuräne leicht zu erkennen. Sie hat kurze kräftige Zähne und ernährt sich hauptsächlich von Krebsen und Muscheln. Sie wird bis etwa einen Meter lang. M, K, A.

Due to its short bulldog-like snout and its dark "Bank-robbers-mask", the brown moray is easy to recognise. It has short, powerful teeth and feeds mostly on crabs and shellfish. It can grow to be about one meter long. M, K, A.

Tigermuräne   Fangtooth moray   Enchelycore anatina

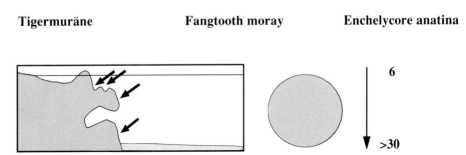

Die langen, dünnen, glasartig durchsichtigen Zähne geben der Tigermuräne ein besonders gefährliches Aussehen. Was sie frißt, ist noch gar nicht bekannt, die Zähne lassen aber auf einen Tintenfisch-Spezialisten schließen. An manchen Tauchbasen wird die Art auch Leopardenmuräne oder Krokodilsmuräne genannt. Sie wird etwas über einen Meter lang. M, K, A.

The long, thin, seethrough glass-like teeth give the fangtooth moray a remarkably dangerous appearance. What it eats, is not yet known, but the teeth indicate an octopus specialist. On many diving bases the species is also known as leopard moray or crocodile moray. It grows to just over one meter long. M, K;A.

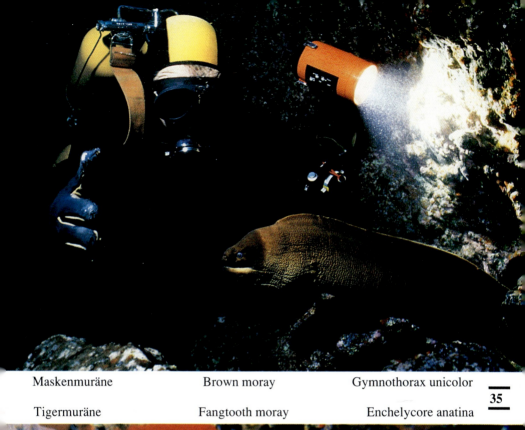

| Maskenmuräne | Brown moray | Gymnothorax unicolor |
| Tigermuräne | Fangtooth moray | Enchelycore anatina |

Zauberaale   Sorcerer Eels   Nettastomidae

Spitzkopf-Zauberaal   Sharpnose sorcerer eel   Faciolella oxyrhyncha

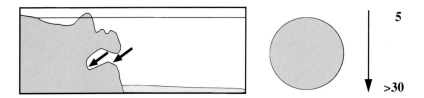

Jungtiere (bis etwa 30 cm) des Spitzkopf-Zauberaals leben in Höhlen im flachen Wasser (ab etwa 5 m). Erwachsene Zauberaale (bis 65 cm) wurden bisher nur in mehreren hundert Meter Tiefe gefangen. M, K.

Young animals (up to more or less 30 cm) of the sharpnose sorcerer eel live in caves in shallow water (from about 5 m). Adult sharpnose sorcerer eels (up to 65 cm) have hithero only been caught in depths of over one hundred meters. M, K.

Schlangenaale   Snake Eels   Ophichthidae

Goldgefleckter Schlangenaal   Golden-spotted snake eel   Myrichthys pardalis
Flossenloser Schlangenaal   Finless snake eel   Apterichthus caecus

Schlangenaale werden häufig mit Seeschlangen verwechselt, aber die gibt es nur im Indopazifik. Der bleistiftdünne Flossenlose Schlangenaal (kleines Bild) sieht eigentlich eher wie ein Wurm aus als wie ein Fisch. Tagsüber ist er völlig im Sand vergraben, nur nachts steckt er den Kopf aus dem Boden heraus: M, K, A.
Der Goldgefleckte Schlangenaal ist tagaktiv und kriecht tatsächlich wie eine Schlange am Boden im Bereich von etwa 3-15 m. K.

Snake eels are frequently mistaken for sea snakes, but these only exist in the Indo-Pacific. The pencil-thin finless snake eel (small photo) looks more like a worm than a fish. During the day, it is completly buried in the sand, and only at night does it stick its head out. M, K, A.
The golden-spotted snake eel is day-active and really crawls like a snake on the bottom at a depth of about 3 to 15 m. K.

Spitzkopf-Zauberaal	Sharpnose sorcerer eel	Faciolella oxyrhyncha▲
Goldgefleckter Schlangenaal	Golden-spotted snake eel	Myrichthys pardalis▼
Flossenloser Schlangenaal	Finless snake eel	Apterichthus caecus▼

Meerale Conger Eels Congridae

Meeraal Conger eel Conger conger

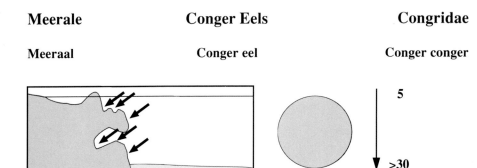

Conger leben an Felsküsten, tags meist in Höhlen und Spalten versteckt; sie können bis zu 3 m lang und mannsdick werden. Männchen werden mit 50-70 cm geschlechtsreif, Weibchen erst mit einer Länge von 2 m. Zur Laichzeit im Hochsommer können große Weibchen bis zu 8 Millionen (!) Eier legen. Manchmal sieht man Conger mit kreisrunden weißen Kringeln am Kopf; den Spuren der Saugnäpfe von Tintenfischen, die sich dagegen gewehrt haben, vom Conger gefressen zu werden. M, K, A.

Conger eels live at rocky shores, during the day hidden in caves and cracks; they can be up to 3 m long and as thick as men. Males are sexually mature at a size of 50-70 cm, females only at a size of 2 m. At spawning time in mid-summer, large females may lay up to 8 million (!) eggs. Sometimes one can see congers which have circular white rings on their head; these are marks left by the suction cups of octopuses who tried to avoid being eaten by a conger. M, K, A.

Balearenaal Golden balearic conger Ariosoma balearicum

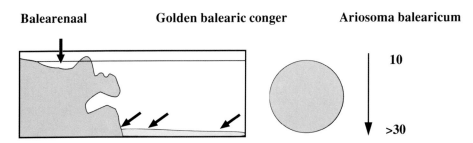

Der Balearenaal ist sozusagen die kleine Sandbodenversion des Congers. Er wird nur 40 cm groß. Tags ist er im Sand vergraben. Nachts schwimmt er dicht über dem Sandboden. Erschreckt man ihn, gräbt er sich blitzschnell mit einigen Schlängelbewegungen rückwärts in den Sand ein. M, K, A.

The golden balearic conger is, one may say, a sandy bottom version of the conger. It only reaches 40 cm in length. During the day it is buried in the sand. At night, it swims close to the bottom. If it is frightened, it buries itself in the sand as quick as lightning with a backwards snake-like movement. M, K, A.

| Meeraal | Conger eel | Conger conger |
| Balearenaal | Golden balearic conger | Ariosoma balearicum |

Meerale   Conger Eels   Congridae

Röhrenaal   Garden eel   Heteroconger longissimus

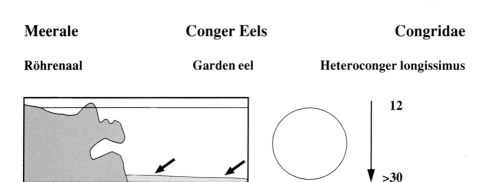

Röhrenaale sind die einzigen "festsitzenden" Wirbeltiere. Sie können ihre mit einem Sekret der Schwanzspitzen-Drüse verfestigte Röhre im Sand zwar auch verlassen, tun es aber nur selten. Tags schnappen sie nach vorbei treibendem Plankton, nachts schlafen sie tief in ihren Röhren. Morgens wird als erstes mit vehementen Schlängelbewegungen der in die Röhre gerieselte Sand wieder herausbefördert. Die Art lebt auf beiden Seiten des Atlantiks. M, K.

Garden eels are the only "sedentary" vertebrates. They can leave their tubes, that are solidified with a secretion of glands at the tip of the tail, but usually they do not do so. During the day, they pick at drifting plankton, and at night they sleep deep down in their tubes. At dawn, the first thing they do is to throw out the sand, which has trickled into their tubes, with a vehement snake-like movement. The species lives on both sides of the Atlantic, in the Eastern Atlantic at Madeira, the Canaries and off the coast of Senegal. M, K.

Großaugen-Meeraal   Bigeye conger   Paraconger macrops

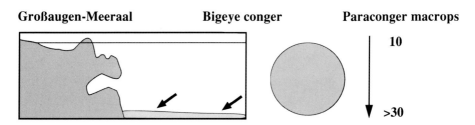

Nicht nur die großen Augen, sondern auch die auffallend dicken Lippen sind ein gutes Erkennungsmerkmal für den Großaugen-Meeraal. Nachts verläßt er die Röhre im Sandboden, in der er sich tags verborgen hält, und geht auf die Jagd nach Fischen und Tintenfischen. Er wird bis 50 cm lang. M, A.

Not only the big eyes, but also the strikingly thick lips are good features to recognise the bigeye conger. At night, it leaves its hole in the sand in which it hides during the day, and goes hunting for fish and octopus. It can reach a length of up to 50 cm. M, A.

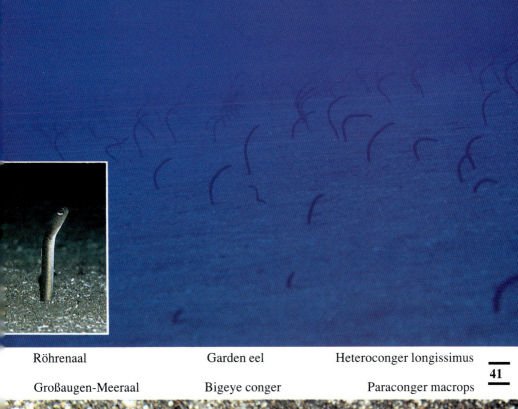

Röhrenaal	Garden eel	Heteroconger longissimus
Großaugen-Meeraal	Bigeye conger	Paraconger macrops

Halbschnäbler	Halfbeaks	Hemirhamphidae
Halbschnäbler	Halfbeak	Hemirhamphus balao
Hornhechte	Needlefish	Belonidae
Hornhecht	Garfish	Belone belone

Halbschnäbler und Hornhechte werden meistens verwechselt. Sie sehen sich nicht nur sehr ähnlich, sondern haben auch noch eine ganz ähnliche Lebensweise. Beide Arten schwimmen in kleinen Gruppen oder einzeln dicht unter der Wasseroberfläche. Daß bei den Halbschnäblern der Oberkiefer kurz ist und nur die untere Hälfte des Maules lang ausgezogen ist, während bei den Hornhechten beide Kiefer verlängert sind, sieht man nur wenn man ganz dicht an die Tiere herankommt. Ein besseres Unterscheidungsmerkmal ist die Position von Rücken und Afterflosse: bei Hornhechten beginnen sie ganz genau auf gleicher Höhe, bei den Halbschnäblern beginnt die Afterflosse erst ein Stück weit hinter der Rückenflosse. Hornhecht M, K, A. Halbschnäbler M, K.

Halfbeaks and needlefish are often mistaken for one another. Not only do they look alike, they also lead very similar lives. Both species swim in small schools or alone close to the surface. Only when one comes up close to these animals is it one can see that the halfbeak has a short upper jaw and only the lower half of its mouth is drawn-out, whereas both of the needlefishes jaws are elongated.
A characteristic to tell them apart is the position of the dorsal and anal fin: in the needlefish's case they both begin at exactly the same level, in the halfbeak's case the anal fin starts a bit further back than the dorsal fin. Needlefish M, K, A.
Halfbeaks M, K.

| Halbschnäbler | Halfbeak | Hemirhamphus balao |
| Hornhecht | Garfish | Belone belone |

Dorsche Codfish Gadidae

Großer Gabeldorsch Larger forkbeard Phycis phycis

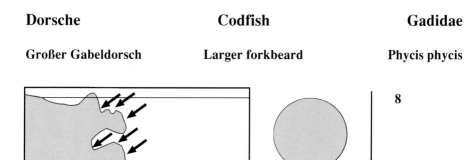

An den langen, gabelförmig gespaltenen Bauchflossen ist der Gabeldorsch leicht zu erkennen. Mit Ihnen tastet er nach Nahrung. Tags steht er an dunklen Orten (in Höhlen oder unter großen Steinen versteckt), nachts geht er auf die Jagd. Bei den Azoren ist er einer der häufigsten großen Küstenfische. Der Große Gabeldorsch wird bis zu 15 Jahre alt. M, K, A.

It is easy to recognise the forkbeard, due to its long forked pelvic fins. With them, it searches for food. During the daytime it lies in dark places (in caves or under large stones), at night it goes out to hunt. In the Azores it is one of the commonest coastal fishes. The larger forkbeard can reach an age of 15 years. M, K, A.

Gefleckte Quappe Spotted rockling Gaidropsarus guttatus

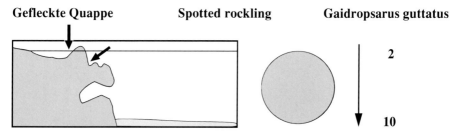

Die erste Rückenflosse der Quappen ist zu einem Sinnesorgan umgestaltet. Die Flossenstrahlen sind sehr kurz und stehen in einer Grube. Die Flosse führt dauernd eine sehr schnelle Schlängelbewegung durch, mit der ein Wasserstrom in diese Grube gezogen wird. Spezielle Sinneszellen testen dann die Geruchsstoffe in diesem Wasserstrom. Tags ist die Gefleckte Quappe meistens unter Steinen versteckt. Sie wird bis zu 25 cm lang. M, K, A.

The rockling's first dorsal fin is modified into a sensory organ. The rays of the fin are very short and lie in a groove. The fin goes through a fast wriggling movement which draws water into this groove. Special sensory cells then test the odorous substances in the water current. During most of the day, the spotted rockling is hidden under rocks. It grows up to 25 cm in length. M, K, A.

| Großer Gabeldorsch | Larger forkbeard | Phycis phycis |
| Gefleckte Quappe | Spotted rockling | Gaidropsarus guttatus |

45

Ährenfische   Sand Smelts   Atherinidae

Ährenfisch   Sand smelt   Atherina presbyter

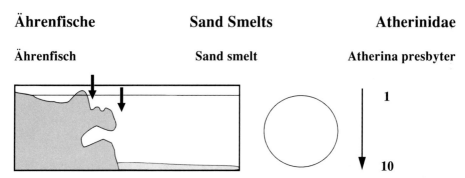

Ährenfische werden häufig mit Sardinen verwechselt. Sie haben aber keinen silbrigen Körper, sondern nur ein silbriges Längsband. Außerdem haben sie nicht eine, sondern zwei Rückenflossen. Ährenfische stehen oft in riesigen Schwärmen im flachen Wasser. Es sind wichtige Futterfische für viele großen Raubfische. M, K, A.

Sand smelts are often mistaken for sardines. They do not have silvery bodies, however, they have a silvery longitudinal stripe. Apart from this, they do not have one, but two dorsal fins. Sand smelts are often found in enormous schools of fish in shallow water. They are important food for many larger predatory fish. M, K, A.

Trompetenfische   Trumpetfish   Aulostomidae

Trompetenfisch   Trumpetfish   Aulostomus strigosus

In der Familie Trompetenfische gibt es nur drei Arten. Aulostomus strigosus lebt im ganzen subtropischen und tropischen Ostatlantik. Trompetenfische sind Raubfische, die kleine Fische und Krebse fressen. Mit ihrem dünnen, lang ausgezogenen Maul kommen sie auch in enge Spalten. Trompetenfische lauern oft bewegungslos kopfabwärts dicht an senkrechten Strukturen. M, K.

There are only three species in the trumpetfish family. Aulostomus strigosus live in all of the Eastern Atlantic, subtropical and tropical. Trumpetfish are predators that feed on small fish and crabs. The long, thin, elongated snout enables them to reach into narrow cracks. Trumpetfish often lurk motionless, with their heads pointing down, close to vertical structures. M, K.

| Ährenfisch | Sand smelt | Atherina presbyter |
| Trompetenfisch | Trumpetfish | Aulostomus strigosus |

Seenadeln und Seepferdchen   Pipefish and Seahorses   Syngnathidae

Langschnäuziges Seepferdchen   Seahorse   Hippocampus ramulosus
Große Seenadel   Great pipefish Syngnathus acus

Bei Seenadeln und Seepferdchen tragen die Männchen die Eier in einer Bruttasche oder Falte am Bauch. Anstelle von Schuppen ist der Körper mit Knochenringen und Halbringen geschützt. Mit ihren langen röhrenförmigen Schnauzen saugen Seenadeln und Seepferdchen kleine Tiere auf wie mit einer Pipette. Beim Seepferdchen dauert die "Tragzeit" drei bis fünf Wochen.
Seepferdchen können bis zu 16 cm groß werden. Die Große Seenadel wird bis zu 46 cm lang. Beide Arten M, K, A.

It is the male pipefish or seahorse who carries the eggs in a brooding pouch or in a belly fold. The body is protected by rings and half rings of bone instead of by scales. Pipefish and seahorses use the long, tube-shaped snout to suck up small animals as if with a pipette. In the seahorse's case, the pregnancy lasts for three to five weeks. Seahorses can grow up to 16 cm. The great pipefish can reach 46 cm in length. Both species M, K, A.

Langschnäuziges Seepferdchen   Seahorse   Hippocampus ramulosus ▶
Große Seenadel   Great pipefish   Syngnathus acus ▼

Schnepfenfische   Snipefish   Macroramphosidae

Schnepfenfisch   Snipefish   Macroramphosus scolopax

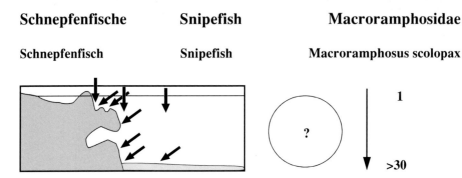

Mit ihren langgezogenen Schnauzen sind die Schnepfenfische unverwechselbar. Sie leben als Schwarmfische. Jungtiere (bis etwa 10 cm Länge) schwimmen vor allem im freien Wasser, oft in der Nähe von treibenden Algenbüscheln, ältere Tiere leben über Felsboden. M,K,A

The snipefish are unmistakeble due to their very long snouts. They live in schools. Young animals (up to about 10 cm long) are mostly found in mid-water, frequently close to drifting sea-weed, older animals live on rocky bottoms. M, K, A.

Heringe   Herrings   Clupeidae

Ohrensardine   Gilt Sardinella   Sardinella aurita

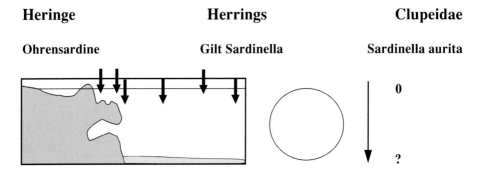

Kleine Schwärme der Ohrensardine schwimmen manchmal in großen Schwärmen von Ährenfischen (Seite 48) mit und fallen dann duch ihre besonders silbrige Farbe auf. Gelegentlich bilden die Ohrensardinen selbst so große und dichte Schwärme, daß man den nur einen Meter entfernten Tauchpartner nicht mehr sieht. M, K.

Small schools of gilt sardinella sometimes swim in big schools of sand smelts (page 48) and are then conspicuous due to their very silvery shine. Occasionally the gilt sardinella alone make up such a big and thick school, that one may be only one meter away from one's diving buddy and still not be able to him. M, K.

| Schnepfenfisch | Snipefish | Macroramphosus scolopax |
| Ohrensardine | Gilt sardinella | Sardinella aurita |

Barrakudas   Barracudas   Sphyraenidae

Gestreifter Barrakuda   Striped barracuda   Sphyraena viridensis

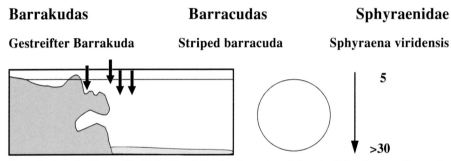

Barrakudas sind hechtähnliche Raubfische. Jungtiere leben in Schwärmen, ältere als Einzelgänger. Typisch für den Gestreiften Barrakuda sind die dunklen Querbänder. Ob es bei Madeira, den Kanaren und den Azoren noch eine zweite Art gibt, ist eher zweifelhaft. Berichte über den Großen Barrakuda (ohne Querbänder aber ev. mit großen unregelmäßig schwarzen Flecken) sind vermutlich Verwechslungen mit dem Gestreiften Barrakuda. M, K, A.

Barracudas are predatory fish similar to pikes. Young animals live in schools, whereas older ones are normally solitary fish. The dark diagonal stripes are typical of the striped barracuda. Whether a second species of barracuda exists at Madeira, Canaries or Azores is somewhat doubtful. Reports of greater barracuda (which has irregular black patches instead of diagonal stripes) are probably due to striped barracudas which were mistaken for greater barracudas. M, K, A.

Meeräschen   Mullets   Mugilidae

Dicklippige Meeräsche   Boxlip mullet   Oedalechilus labeo

Meeräschen sind Schwarmfische, die ihre Nahrung wie Staubsauger aufsammeln. Mit ihren dicken ledrigen Lippen fahren sie über Schlammboden, Sand, Pflanzen und Fels und sieben das Eingesaugte nach Kleintieren durch. Die verschiedenen Arten sind sehr schwer zu unterscheiden. Diese Art ist nur von Madeira mit Sicherheit nachgewiesen, es gibt aber bei den Azoren und bei den Kanaren ähnliche Arten.

Mullets are schooling fish which gather their food somewhat like a vaccum cleaner. They use their thick leathery lips to guide themselves over muddy bottoms, sand, plants and gravel and sieve the sucked-up water for small animals. The different species are very difficult to distinguish. The species shown in the photo has been recorded with certainty only at Madeira; there are several similar species at the Canaries and the Azores.

| Gestreifter Barrakuda | Striped barracuda | Sphyraena viridensis |
| Dicklippige Meeräsche | Boxlip mullet | Oedalechilus labeo |

Eberfische   Boarfish   Caproidae

Eberfisch   **Boarfish**   **Capros aper**

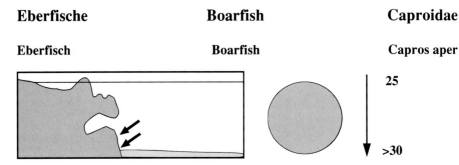

Normalerweise kommen Eberfische erst ab etwa 50 m Tiefe vor, am häufigsten in 100 bis 400 m Tiefe, und auch in Netzen, die aus 600 m Tiefe kamen, hingen noch Eberfische. Als Taucher wird man ihnen also nur selten begegnen. Die beiden Fotos entstanden während eines Nachttauchgangs bei den Azoren, bei dem aus unbekannten Gründen ein dichter Schwarm von mehreren tausend Eberfischen in nur 25 m Tiefe angetroffen wurde. M, K, A.

One can normally find Boarfish in waters deeper than 50 m, usually at depths between 100 and 400 m, although they also have been found in nets which came from depths of 600 m. Therefor, divers seldom come across them. Both these photos were taken during a night dive at the Azores during which, for an unknown reason, a tight school of more than a thousand Boarfish were encountered in a depth of only 25 m. M, K, A.

Heringskönige   Dories   Zeidae

Heringskönig   **John dory**   **Zeus faber**

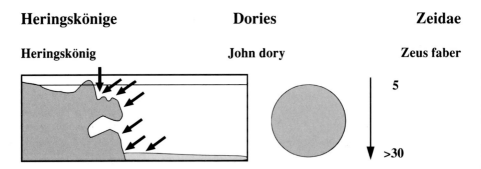

Langsam schwebend nähert sich der Heringskönig seinen Beutetieren (kleinen Fischen und Krebsen) und saugt sie dann plötzlich mit seinem sehr weit vorstreckbaren Maul ein. Heringskönige können bis zu 70 cm lang werden. M, K, A.

Slowly hovering, the john dory approaches his prey (small fish and crabs) and then suddenly sucks them into its mouth that can be streched far out. John dorys reach 70 cm in length. M, K, A.

| Eberfisch | Boarfish | Capros aper |
| Heringskönig | John dory | Zeus faber |

Zackenbarsche   Groupers   Serranidae

Makaronesen-Zackenbarsch   Comb grouper   Mycteroperca fusca

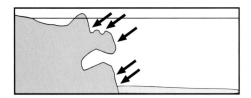 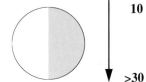

Durch eine systematische Untersuchung der Zackenbarsche des Ostatlantiks wurde 1991 festgestellt, daß diese Art nur bei Madeira, den Kanaren und den Azoren vorkommt, also den sogenannten Makaronesischen Inseln (siehe Einleitung). Von der nahe verwandten Art Mycteroperca rubra, die im Mittelmeer und an der afrikanischen Festlandsküste lebt, unterscheidet sie sich in einem Merkmal, das man beim lebenden Tier gar nicht sieht: sie hat weniger Dornen auf der Innenseite der Kiemenbögen. Gelbfärbung von Tieren einer sonst anders gefärbten Art ("Xanthochromismus") ist bei Fischen etwa so häufig wie ausnahmsweise Schwarzfärbung ("Melanismus") bei Säugetieren. Das im kleinen Bild gezeigte Tier ist an den weißen Flecken an den Lippen leicht individuell zu erkennen. Rainer Waschkewitz von Madeira konnte zehn Jahre lang beobachten, daß dieses Individuum immer im April aus der Bucht von Kap Garajau verschwand und dann im September oder Oktober wieder zurückkam. Daß viele Fische jährliche Wanderungen durchführen, ist bekannt, aber daß ein individueller Fisch wie ein Zugvogel jedes Jahr immer wieder an den gleichen Ort zurückkommt, war bis dahin nicht bekannt gewesen. M, K, A.

During a systematical study of the groupers of the Eastern Atlantic, it was found that this species exists only in Madeira, the Canaries and the Azores, therefore only in the so called Macaronesian islands (see introduction). This species differs from a similar one, Mycteroperca rubra, which lives in the Mediteranean Sea and just off the African coast, in a way that is not visible in live animals. It has fewer spines on the inner side of the gill arches.
Yellow colour in fishes that belong to a species normally coloured differently ("Xanthochromism") is as common as the exceptional black colour ("Melanism") in some mammals. The animal shown in the small photo could be easily recognised due to the white patches on its lips. Rainer Waschewitz from Madeira has observed this individual animal for ten years, and noted that it disappeared from Garajau Bay each year in April, to reappear in September or October the same year. It was already known that many fish perform annual migrations, but it had not been known until then that like a migratory bird an individual fish would each year return to the same place. M, K, A.

Zackenbarsche — Groupers — Serranidae

Brauner Zackenbarsch — Dusky grouper — Epinephelus marginatus

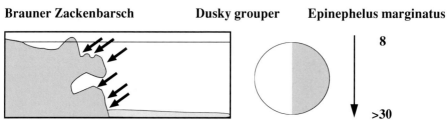

Mit bis zu 1,6 m Länge ist diese Art einer der größten Küstenfische. Bis vor kurzem hieß sie noch E. guaza. Große Exemplare sind 40 bis 50 Jahre alt. Wie alle großen Zackenbarsche (Gattungen Epinephelus und Mycteroperca) ist auch diese Art ein Geschlechtswechsler: geschlechtsreif mit etwa 40 cm und zuerst Weibchen, mit einer Länge von etwa 80 cm dann Umwandlung zum Männchen. M, K, A.

With a length of up to 1.6 m, the dusky grouper is one of the biggest coastal fish. Until recently this species was known as Epinephalus guaza. Large animals are 40 to 50 years old. As with all big groupers (genus Epinephelus and Mycteroperca) the dusky grouper also changes sex; with a size of about 40 cm, it becomes sexually mature and, to start with, female; when it reaches a size of about 80 cm, it changes to male sex. M, K, A.

Schriftbarsch — Painted comber — Serranus scriba

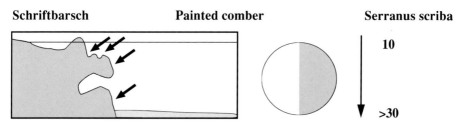

Der Schriftbarsch verdankt seinen Namen den wie arabische Schriftzeichen aussehenden blauen Streifen auf dem Kiemendeckel. Wie alle Arten der Gattung Serranus ist er ein Simultanhermaphrodit, das heißt jedes Tier ist gleichzeitig voll funktionsfähiges Männchen und Weibchen. Zwei Tiere geben immer ein Paar; sie müssen sich also "nur" noch darüber einig werden, wer beim gemeinsamen Ablaichen die Eier und wer die Spermien ausstößt. M, K, A.

The painted comber gets its name from the blue markings on its gill cover which resemble arabic letters. As all the species of the genus Serranus, it is a simultaneousl hermaphrodite, which means that each animal is at the same time a fully functional male and female. Two animals always make a pair. They must, therefore, "only" decide who shall lay the eggs and who shall eject the sperm. M, K, A.

| Brauner Zackenbarsch | Dusky grouper | Epinephelus marginatus |
| Schriftbarsch | Painted comber | Serranus scriba |

Zackenbarsche — Groupers — Serranidae

Schwarzschwanz-Sägebarsch — **Blacktail comber** — *Serranus atricauda*
Beutelbarsch — **Brown comber** — *Serranus hepatus*

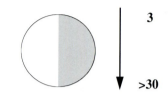

Der Schwarzschwanz-Sägebarsch verdankt seinen Namen den schwarzen Schwanzspitzen (kleines Bild). Allerdings gibt es von dieser Art gelegentlich auch eine Farbvariante, die eine völlig andere Körperfarbe hat (unten rechts). M, K, A.

Ob der Beutelbarsch wirklich bei den Kanaren vorkommt, oder ob es sich um eine Falschmeldung handelt, ist noch unklar; das Foto stammt von der Algarve. K?

The blacktail comber owes its name to its black tipped tail fin (small picture). One can occasionaly come across a colour varity of this species, which has a completely different body colours (bottom right) M, K, A.

Whether the brown comber really exists at the Canaries, or whether this is a false report, is still uncertain; the photo was taken at the Algarve. K?

Beutelbarsch — Brown comber — *Serranus hepatus*

Schwarzschwanz-Sägebarsch Blacktail comber Serranus atricauda

Zackenbarsche · Groupers · Serranidae

Roter Fahnenbarsch · Swallowtail seaperch · Anthias anthias

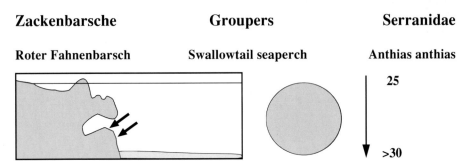

25
>30

Die Fahnenbarsche bilden eine eigene Unterfamilie innerhalb der Zackenbarsche. Die meisten der über hundert Arten leben in den Tropen. Der Rote Fahnenbarsch, der an den enorm verlängerten Bauchflossen leicht zu erkennen ist, wird bis 26 cm lang, aber in der Regel sieht man Tiere von etwa 10 cm Länge. Er steht meistens in kleinen Gruppen vor Höhlen oder Felsüberhängen. M, K, A.

The swallowtail seaperches form a seperate subfamily within the groupers. Of over one hundred species, most live in the tropics. The swallowtail seaperch, which is easily recognised due to its very elongated pelvic fin, grows to be up to 26 cm long, although as a rule one sees animals of about 10 cm long. It is normally found in small groups in front of caves or cliff overhangs. M, K, A.

Kardinalbarsche · Cardinalfish · Apogonidae

Meerbarbenkönig · Cardinalfish · Apogon imberbis

4
>30

Bei den Kardinalbarschen tragen die Männchen die Eier im Maul, bis die Jungen schlüpfen. Eiertragende Männchen erkennt man an den auffällig nach unten vorgewölbten Kehlen. Das Foto zeigt ein typisches Verhalten vieler Höhlenfische, den Licht-Rücken-Reflex: die Tiere drehen häufig den Rücken zum Licht und wenn der Boden einer Höhle heller ist als die Decke, schwimmen einige Tiere mit dem Rücken nach unten. M, K, A.

In the cardinalfish's case, it is the male who carries the eggs in its mouth, until the young hatch. Egg-carrying males are recognised by their strikingly bulging throats. The photo shows a typical behaviour of many cave-dwelling fish: the animals often (but not always) turn their backs to the light and, if the bottom of a cave is lighter than the ceiling, swim upside down. M, K, A.

| Roter Fahnenbarsch | Swallowtail seaperch | Anthias anthias |
| Meerbarbenkönig | Cardinalfish | Apogon imberbis |

Großaugen   Bigeyes   Priacanthidae

Glasauge   Glasseye   Heteropriacanthus cruentatus
Atlantischer Großaugenbarsch   Atlantic bigeye   Priacanthus arenatus

Mit ihren riesigen, stark reflektierenden Augen sind die Großaugenbarsche typische nachtaktive Fische. Die meisten der 18 Arten in dieser Familie leben in den Tropen. Die beiden abgebildeten Arten leben sowohl im östlichen als auch im westlichen Atlantik. Der Atlantische Großaugenbarsch dringt etwas weiter nach Norden vor als das Glasauge. Beide Arten können ihre Farbe von rot über rot-gefleckt zu silbern wechseln. Die beiden Arten unterscheiden sich etwas in der Körperform: das Glasauge ist hochrückiger. Am leichtesten sind sie aber in der Färbung zu unterscheiden: nur der Atlantische Großaugenbarsch hat einen schwarzen Fleck am Ansatz der Bauchflossen. Glasauge: M, K. Atlantischer Großaugenbarsch M, K, A.

With their enormous, strongly reflecting eyes, bigeyes are typical nocturnal fish. Most of the 18 species in this family live in the tropics. Both the species which are photographed here, live not only in the Eastern Atlantic but also the Western Atlantic. The atlantic bigeye penetrates a bit further north than the glasseye. Both species can change their colour from red through red-spotted to silvery. There is a difference between species in the shape of the body; the glasseye has a higher back. The easiest way to differentiate them, however, is in their colour: only the atlantic bigeye has a black spot at the base of the pelvic fin. Glasseye M, K. Atlantic bigeye M, K, A.

| Glasauge | Glasseye | Heteropriacanthus cruentatus |
| Atlantischer Großaugenbarsch | Atlantic bigeye | Priacanthus arenatus |

Meerbrassen	Breams	Sparidae
Zweibindenbrasse Geißbrasse	Two-banded bream White bream	Diplodus vulgaris Diplodus sargus

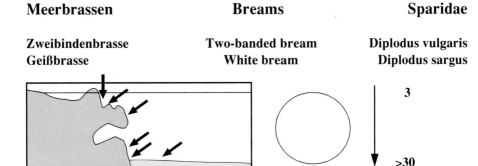

Je nach Ernährungsweise haben die Meerbrassen ganz unterschiedliche Gebisse mit verschieden vielen Schneidezähnen, Eckzähnen und Mahlzähnen (also Gebisse, wie sie Säugetiere haben). Die meisten Fische haben dagegen ein Gebiß aus nur einer Sorte von (in der Regel kegelförmigen) Zähnen, die höchstens in der Größe unterschiedlich sind. Die beiden hier abgebildeten Brassenarten sind die häufigsten im Ostatlantik und gehören zu den häufigsten Küstenfisch überhaupt. Sie werden etwa 45 cm groß, meistens sieht man aber Exemplare von 20-30 cm Länge. Im Alter von zwei Jahre, mit einer Länge von 15-20 cm werden sie geschlechtsreif. Zweibindenbrasse M, K. Geißbrasse M, K, A.

According to their feeding habits, breams can have quite different yaws, with a different number of incisor-like, canine and molar teeth (yaws like those of mammals). Most fish, in contrast, have only one kind of teeth (as a rule cone shaped) which differ in size at most. The two breams which are shown here are the commonest in the Eastern Atlantic and belong to the most common coastal fish of all. They can reach a size of 45 cm, although mostly one sees animals which are 20-30 cm long. At an age of two years, with a size of 15-20 cm, they become sexually mature.
Two-banded bream M, K. White ream M, K, A.

| Zweibindenbrasse | Two-banded bream | Diplodus vulgaris |
| Geißbrasse | White bream | Diplodus sargus |

Meerbrassen   Breams   Sparidae

Bänderbrasse   **Zebra bream**   **Diplodus cervinus**

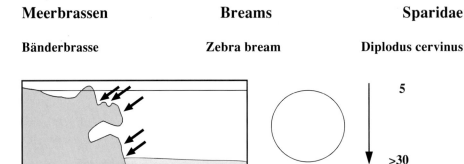

Die meisten Meerbrassen sind hochrückige schlanke Fische, die in mehr oder weniger großen Gruppen dicht über dem Boden schwimmen. Die Bänderbrasse ist wegen ihrer Färbung unverwechselbar. Diese Art kommt auch im westlichen (aber nicht im östlichen) Mittelmeer vor. Sie wird bis 55 cm groß. M, K.

Most breams are slim, high-backed fish, which swim in more or less big schools close to the bottom. The zebra bream is unmistakeable due to its colour. This species also lives in the Western (but not in the Eastern) Mediterranean Sea. It can reach a length of 55 cm. M, K.

Streifenbrasse   **Black bream**   **Spondyliosoma cantharus**

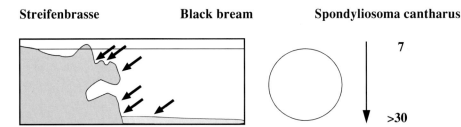

Die Streifenbrasse ist häufig viel heller gefärbt als auf dem Foto, das wahrscheinlich ein brutpflegendes (dunkles) Männchen zeigt; die gelben Streifen sind dann weniger auffällig und aus größerer Entfernung nicht zu sehen. Während die Bänderbrasse in kleinen Gruppen oder alleine schwimmt, bildet die Streifenbrasse Schwärme von manchmal vielen hundert Tieren. Zur Laichzeit (April bis Juli) graben die Männchen flache Gruben im Sand, in die die Weibchen die winzigen klebrigen Eier legt. M, K.

The black bream often is much lighter than the one in the photo, which probably shows brood-guarding (dark) male; the yellow stripes are then less striking and are invisible from a greater distance. Whereas the zebra breams swim in small schools or alone, the black breams form schools of sometimes many hundred animals. During the spawning season (April to July), the males dig shallow pits in the sand, into which the females lay the minute sticky eggs. M, K.

| Bänderbrasse | Zebra bream | Diplodus cervinus |
| Streifenbrasse | Black bream | Spondyliosoma cantharus |

Meerbrassen   Breams   Sparidae

Goldstriemen   Cow bream   Sarpa salpa

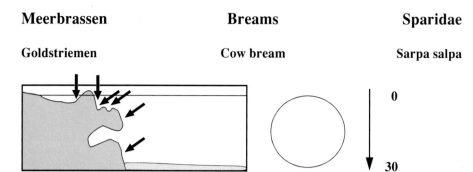

Der englische Name "Kuhbrasse" ist recht zutreffend für diese Art. In Schwärmen ziehen die Tiere durch zum Teil ganz flaches Wasser und weiden Pflanzen ab. Sie werden bis zu 45 cm groß, aber meistens sieht man Tiere von etwa 20 cm Länge. Mit dieser Größe werden sie geschlechtsreif und zwar als erstes Männchen; später wechseln sie das Geschlecht und werden Weibchen. M, K, A.

The name cow bream is perfect for this species. Its swims in schools in sometimes very shallow water and there grazes on plants. They can reach 45 cm in length, but as a rule, one finds animals with a length of about 20 cm. At this size they reach sexuall maturity and first are male; later on they change sex and become female. M, K, A.

Gelbstriemen   Bogue   Boops boops

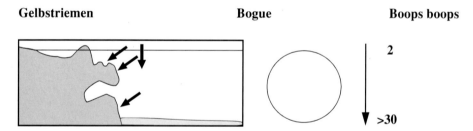

Gelbstriemen stehen in Schwärmen von bis zu vielen hunderten Tieren im freien Wasser an Felsküsten. Sie ernähren sich hauptsächlich von Plankton, nehmen aber auch Nahrung vom Boden auf. Aus größerer Entfernung sehen sie silbrig aus. Erst wenn man ganz nahe ist, erkennt man zwei bis drei dünne braungelbe Längslinien. Gelbstriemen werden bis zu 6 Jahre alt. M, K, A.

Bogues swim in schools of up to many hundred animals in mid-water near rocky shores. They mainly feed on plankton, but also gather food from the sea-bed. From further away they appear silvery. Only when one is very close does one recognise two to three thin yellowy-brown horizontal lines. Bogues reach an age of up to six years. M, K, A.

| Goldstriemen | Cow bream | Sarpa salpa |
| Gelbstriemen | Bogue | Boops boops |

Meerbrassen Breams Sparidae

Achselfleckbrasse Axillary bream Pagellus acarne

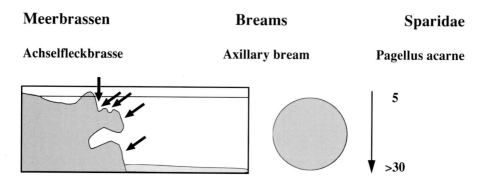

In Küstennähe sieht man meistens nur Jungfischschwärme von dieser Art. Erwachsene Tiere leben in bis zu 200 m Wassertiefe. An ihren deutlichen schwarzen Achselflecken ist diese bis 45 cm groß werdende Art gut zu erkennen. M, K, A.

Near to the shore one generally sees only schools of young fish of this species. Adult animals live in depths of up to 200 m. Due to their distinct black axil spots, this species, which grows to be up to 45 cm long, is easily recognised.

Marmorbrasse Striped bream Lithognathus mormyrus

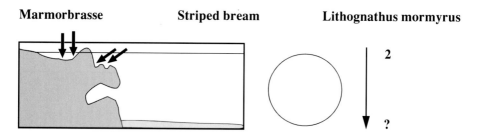

Auch die bis zu 30 cm großen Marmorbrassen sind Schwarmfische. Am häufigsten sieht man sie über Sand und Schlammboden. Seltsamerweise ist diese Art sowohl im Mittelmeer als auch bei den Kanarischen Inseln recht häufig, aber von Madeira bisher nicht bekannt. Sollten Sie also ein Foto von dieser Art von Madeira oder von den Azoren haben, schicken Sie es bitte an die in der Einleitung angegebene Adresse. K.

The up to 30 cm long striped bream is also a schooling fish. Normally they are found over muddy and sandy bottoms. Oddly enough, this species is not only common in the Mediteranean but also in the Canaries, although it is not yet known to exist at Madeira. If you possibly have a photo of this species, taken at Madeira or the Azores, please send it to the address given in the introduction. K.

| Achselfleckbrasse | Axillary bream | Pagellus acarne |
| Marmorbrasse | Striped bream | Lithognathus mormyrus |

Meerbrassen — Breams — Sparidae

Sackbrasse — **Common bream** — **Pagrus pagrus**

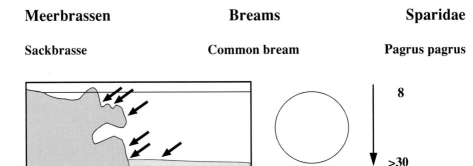

Mit bis zu 80 cm Länge ist die Sackbrasse eine der größten Meerbrassenarten. Jungtiere (kleines Bild) haben auffallend weiße Schwanzspitzen; auch bei älteren Tieren sind sie meistens noch etwas heller als der Rest der Schwanzflosse. Geschlechtsreife mit einer Länge von etwa 25 cm. Ältere Tiere haben ein steileres Kopfprofil als junge und dadurch einen ziemlich massig wirkenden Schädel. Die Hauptnahrung sind Krebse. M, K, A.

With a size of up to 80 cm, the common bream is one of the largest bream species. The tips of young animals' tails (small photo) are a striking white colour; the tips of the adults' tails are also somewhat lighter than the rest of the tail fin. Sexually mature at a length of about 25 cm, adult animals have a steeper head profile than younger animals due to which their heads appear considerably more massive. Crabs are the main nourishment of this species. M, K, A.

Oblada — **Saddled bream** — **Oblada melanura**

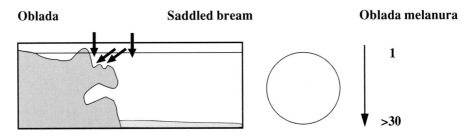

Der weiß umrandete schwarze Fleck auf dem Schwanzstiel ist typisch für diese Art. Die Tiere stehen oft in Schwärmen im freien Wasser an Felsküsten. Die Art wird bis zu 30 cm groß. M, K.

The white border surrounding the black patch on the tail is typical for the species. These animals are often found in schools in mid-water near rocky shores. The species reaches a size of up to 30 cm. M, K.

| Sackbrasse | Common bream | Pagrus pagrus |
| Oblada | Saddled bream | Oblada melanura |

Meerbrassen   Breams   Sparidae

Rotbrasse   **Pandora**   **Pagellus erythrinus**

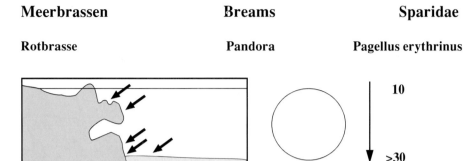

Auf den ersten Blick sehen sich die beiden Brassen auf dieser Seite sehr ähnlich (die langen Rückenflossenstrahlen der Buckelkopfbrasse sieht man nämlich aus der Entfernung nicht). Je länger man hinschaut, desto mehr Unterschiede findet man aber. Die Rotbrasse wird 60 cm groß. M, K

At first sight, both breams on this page look a lot alike (because one cannot see the elongated dorsal fin rays of the lump-headed bream from a distance). But the longer one looks the more differences one finds. The pandora reaches a length of 60 cm. M, K.

Buckelkopfbrasse   **Lump-headed bream**   **Dentex gibbosus**

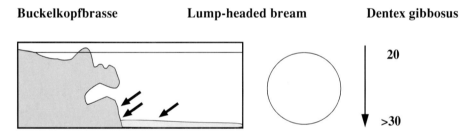

Nur die Jungtiere der Buckelkopfbrasse haben den lang ausgezogenen dritten Rückenflossenstrahl. Im Sporttaucher-Bereich sieht man auch nur Jungtiere: die Erwachsenen leben in Tiefen bis zu 200 m. Der Name kommt daher, daß die Männchen mit zunehmender Größe eine immer dicker werdende kräftige Beule am Kopf entwickeln. M, K.

Only the young animals of the lump-headed bream have the elongated third dorsal fin ray. Within scuba-diving depth, however, one only sees young animals: older animals live in depths of up to 200 m. The name comes from the increasingly thicker lump which the growing males develop on their heads. M, K.

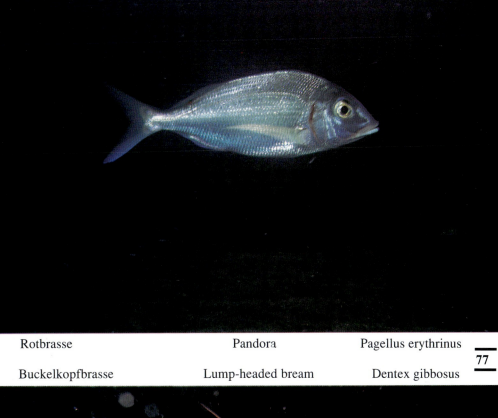

| Rotbrasse | Pandora | Pagellus erythrinus |
| Buckelkopfbrasse | Lump-headed bream | Dentex gibbosus |

Pilotbarsche   Sea Chubs   Kyphosidae

Bermuda-Blaufisch   **Bermuda sea chub**   **Kyphosus sectator**

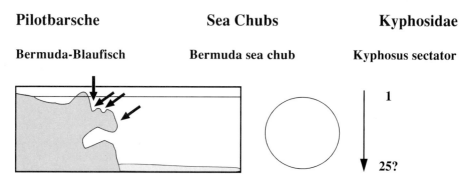

Pilotbarsche fressen Algen und schwimmen in Gruppen, häufig dicht unter der Wasseroberfläche. Außer der im Foto gezeigten Färbung können die Tiere auch noch kurzzeitig eine Schachbrett-ähnliche Musterung annehmen. Die Art lebt auf beiden Seiten des Atlantiks. M, K, A.

Sea chubs eat seaweed and swim in groups, often close to the surface. Apart from the colour shown in the photo, these animals can, for a short time, take on a chess-board pattern. This species lives on both sides of the Atlantic. M, K, A.

Meerbarben   Goatfish   Mullidae

Gestreifte Meerbarbe   **Striped mullet**   **Mullus surmuletus**

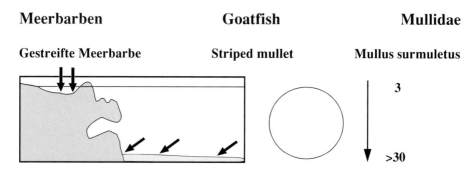

Mit ihren Barteln tasten Meerbarben den Boden nach Freßbarem ab. Manchmal graben sie tiefe Löcher im Sand oder Schlamm. Große Meerbarben werden oft von anderen Fischen begleitet, z.B. Meerjunkern (Seite 96) oder Weitaugenbutten (Seite 130), die nach von den Meerbarben aufgescheuchten Tieren schnappen. Die Barteln können in eine Falte am Kinn eingeklappt werden. Das kleine Bild zeigt die Nachtfärbung. M, K, A.

With its long barbels the goatfish feels the sea-bed for food. Sometimes it digs deep holes in sandy or muddy bottoms. Large goatfish are often accompanied by other fish, rainbow wrasses (page 96), for example, or wide-eyed flounders (page 130), which snap at animals stirred up by the goatfish. The barbels can be tucked away into a fold in the throat region. The small photo shows the nightime colour of the species. M, K, A.

| Bermuda-Blaufisch | Bermuda sea chub | Kyphosus sectator |
| Gestreifte Meerbarbe | Striped mullet | Mullus surmuletus |

Grunzer   Grunts   Haemulidae

Gelbflossengrunzer   **Bastard grunt**   **Pomadasis incisus**

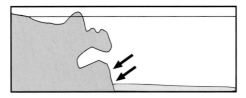 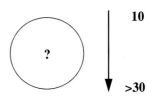

Bei Madeira und den Kanaren ist der Gelbflossengrunzer einer der häufigsten Schwarmfische. Oft sind die Flosen aber nicht ganz so auffällig gefärbt wie im großen Bild, sondern nur leicht gelblich, wie im unteren Bild. Grunzer können bei Bedrohung deutlich hörbare Laute erzeugen, indem sie die Schlundzähne aneinanderreiben. M, K.

At Madeira and the Canaries the bastard grunt is one of the commonest schooling fish. Often, however, the fins are not as strikingly coloured as shown in the big photo, but instead are only slightly yellowish, as in the bottom photo. When threatened, grunts can emit a distictly audible sound by grating their pharyngeal teeth. M, K.

Gelbflossengrunzer   Bastard grunt   Pomadasis incisus ▶

Grunzer — Grunts — Haemulidae

Achtstreifengrunzer — African striped grunt — *Parapristipoma octolineatum*

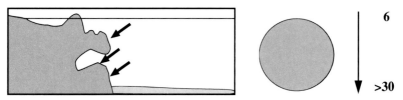

Vier weiße Streifen auf jeder Körperseite haben dem Achtstreifengrunzer seinen Namen gegeben. Er steht meist in kleinen Gruppen an eher dunklen Stellen (Höhleneingängen und Überhängen). Die Art wird bis zu 50 cm lang. M, K.

The african striped grunt gets its name from the four white stripes on each side of its body. It is normally found in small groups in rather dark places (in front of cave entrances and under overhangs). The species grows up to 50 cm long. M, K.

Blaubarsche — Bluefish — Pomatomidae

Blaubarsch — Bluefish — *Pomatomus saltator*

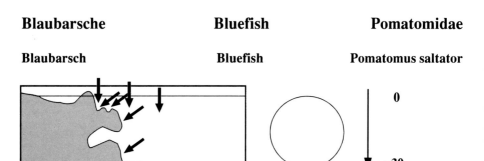

Blaubarsche sind Raubfische die in großen Schwärmen oder einzel jagen. Sie sind als besonders blutrünstig verschrieen. Blaubarsche, die über einen Schwarm Fische herfallen, töten angeblich mehr Tiere als sie fressen können und hinterlassen "eine Wolke von Blut". Der Blaubarsch wird bis zu 110 cm groß. M, K, A.

Bluefish are predatory fish which hunt either in big schools or alone. They are notorious for being particullary blood thirsty. Bluefish, which fall upon a school of fish, allegedly kill more animals than they can eat and leave behind "a cloud of blood". The bluefish can reach a size of 110 cm. M, K, A.

| Achtstreifengrunzer | African striped grunt | Parapristipoma octolineatum |
| Blaubarsch | Bluefish | Pomatomus saltator |

Stachelmakrelen   Jacks   Carangidae

Große Bernsteinmakrele	Amberjack	Seriola dumerili ▶
Kleine Bernsteinmakrele	Almaco jack	Seriola rivoliana ▼

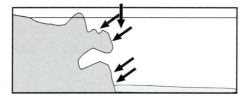 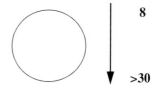

8

>30

Die vier verschiedenen Arten von Bernsteinmakrelen sind schwer zu unterscheiden Auf den ersten Blick sind die beiden abgebildeten Arten recht ähnlich. Die Kleine Bernsteinmakrele ist jedoch etwas hochrückiger und hat länger ausgezogene Rücken- und Afterflossen. Bei Bernsteinmakrelen von über 1m Länge handelt es sich um die Große Bernsteinmakrele (bis 1,9 m lang!). Die anderen drei Arten werden bei weitem nicht so groß. Beide abgebildete Arten: M, K, A.

The four different species of jacks are difficult to distinguish. At first glance, both the photographed species appear quite similar. The almaco jack is somewhat higher-backed and has longer drawn-out dorsal and anal fins. If you see a jack over one meter long, then you can be sure that it is an amberjack (up to 1,9 m long!). The other three species do not grow anything as big. Both species shown: M, K, A.

Stachelmakrelen　　　Jacks　　　Carangidae

Rauchflossenmakrele　　　**Blue runner**　　　**Caranx crysos**

	5
	>30

Die Rauchflossenmakrele ist ein Tier des offenen Meeres und kommt nur selten in Küstennähe. Manchmal schwimmt eine kleine Gruppe dieser Art in großen Schwärmen anderer Stachelmakrelen mit. Sie wird bis 55 cm lang. M?, K?, A.

The blue runner in an open sea animal and seldom comes in near to the shore. Sometimes a small school of this species will swim with a large school of other jacks. They grow to be 55 cm long. M?,K?,A.

Gelbflossen-Stachelmakrele　　　**Guelly jack**　　　**Pseudocaranx dentex**

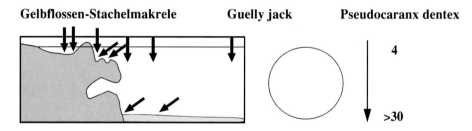

Gelbflossen-Stachelmakrelen ziehen in kleinen Trupps und auch in Schwärmen von mehreren tausend Tieren sowohl durch das offene Meer als auch in Küstennähe. Vor allem Jungtiere (kleines Bild) sieben gerne den Sandboden nach Freßbarem durch. Die Art wird bis zu 80 cm groß. M, K, A.

Guelly jacks travel in small groups and also in schools of more than a thousand animals not only through open water but also near the shore.
Most of the young animals (small photo) like to sieve sandy bottoms for edibles. This species can grow to be up to 80 cm long. M, K, A.

| Rauchflossenmakrele | Blue runner | Caranx crysos |
| Gelbflossen-Stachelmakrele | Guelly jack | Pseudocaranx dentex |

Stachelmakrelen Jacks Carangidae

Gabelmakrele Pompano Trachinotus ovatus

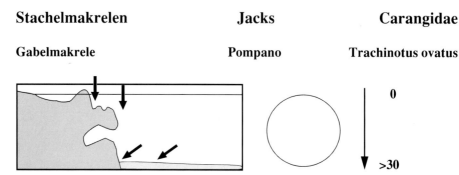

Charakteristisch für die Familie Stachelmakreklen sind zwei kurze kräftige Stacheln vor der Afterflosse, die man aber bei frei schwimmenden Tieren nicht sieht. Junge Gabelmakrelen stehen häufig in kleinen Gruppen dicht unter der Wasseroberfläche in der Brandungszone, Erwachsene (bis 60 cm Länge) leben tiefer über Sand- und Schlammböden. M, K, A.

Characteristical of the jack family are two short, strong spines in front of the anal fin, which, however, one cannot see on swimming animals. Young pompanos can often be found in small groups just under the surface in the area where the surf breaks, adults (up to 60 cm long) live deeper, over sandy and muddy bottoms. M, K, A.

Bastardmakrele Horse mackerel Trachurus picturatus

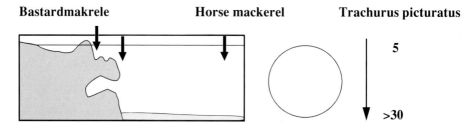

Obwohl sie Makrelen erstaunlich ähnlich sehen, sind Bastardmakrelen keine Makrelenverwandten (Seite 112) sondern Stachelmakrelen. Zu erkennen sind sie an der auffallend geknickten Seitenlinie. Jungfische schwimmen manchmal mit Quallen. Sie manöverieren geschickt zwischen den Tentakeln der Quallen (die für sie selbst durchaus auch gefährlich sind) und sind dadurch vor größeren Raubfeinden geschützt. M, K, A.

Although they look remarkably like makerel, horse makerels are related to jacks. They are recognisable by their conspicuously bent lateral line. Young fish sometimes swim together with jelly-fish. They skillfully manouver between the tentacles of the jelly-fish (for they are themselves in danger of being stung) and are in this way protected from larger predators. M, K, A.

| Gabelmakrele | Pompano | Trachinotus ovatus |
| Bastardmakrele | Horse mackerel | Trachurus picturatus |

Riffbarsche Damselfish Pomacentridae

Atlantischer Mönchsfisch   Atlantic damselfish   Chromis limbata

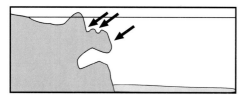 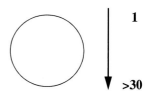

Riffbarsche sind eine artenreiche Familie, zu der z.b. auch die Clownfische der Tropen gehören. Bei Madeira, den Kanaren und den Azoren gibt es nur zwei Arten. Der Atlantische Riffbarsch wurde lange für die gleiche Art wie der Mittelmeer-Riffbarsch (Chromis chromis) gehalten. Die erwachsenen Tiere sind sich auf den ersten Blick auch wirklich recht ähnlich. Einer der vielen kleinen Unterschiede ist z.B. die Färbung der Jungtiere: die Jungtiere des Atlantischen Riffbarschs sind grün gefärbt, während sie beim Mittelmeer-Riffbarsch blau sind. Jungtiere verstecken sich gerne zwischen Seeigelstacheln (kleines Bild unten).
Zur Laichzeit verteidigen Männchen ein Stück leicht überhängender Felswand und balzen vorbeischwimmende Weibchen durch "Signalsprünge" an. Territoriale Männchen (oberes Bild) haben intensivere Farben als nicht-territoriale Männchen oder Weibchen (unten mit Putzergarnele Lysmata grabhami). M, K, A.

Pomacentrids are a family with many species, among them the famous clownfish of the tropics. At Madeira, the Canaries and the Azores, only two species exist.
The atlantic damselfish was long considered the same species as the mediterranean damselfish (Chromis chromis). Adult animals do in fact look very similar at first sight. One of the many small differences is, for example, the colour of the young animals: The young of the atlantic damselfish are a green colour, whereas the mediteranean damselfish's are blue. Young animals like to hide themselves in between sea urchin spines (small photo bottom).
During the spawning season, males defend an area of slightly overhanging rock-face and court passing females with "signal jumps". Territorial males (top photo) have much more intensive colours than non-territorial males or females (below with cleaner shrimp Lysmata grabhami). M, K, A.

Atlantischer Mönchsfisch   Atlantic damselfish   Chromis limbata   **91**

Riffbarsche   Damselfish   Pomacentridae

Neon-Riffbarsch   **Bluefin damselfish**   **Abudefduf luridus**

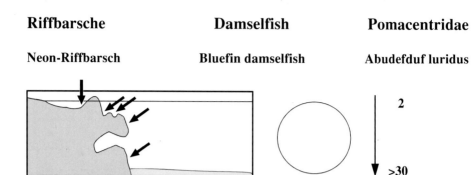

Die systematische Stellung der zweiten Riffbarsch Art ist noch unklar. Wahrscheinlich gehört sie doch nicht in die sehr artenreiche tropische Gattung Abudefduf. Wie beim Atlantischen Mönchsfisch (Seite 86) verteidigen territoriale Männchen ein Stückchen leicht überhängende Felswand, das sie vorher sorgfältig geputzt haben. Weibchen legen ihre Eier an diese Stelle und gehen wieder weg. Das Männchen verteidigt das Gelege und greift dabei manchmal sogar Taucher an. Im oberen Foto ist am linken Bildrand ein Gelege zu sehen.
Mit zunehmender Größe ändern die Jungfische ihre Farbe mehrmals. Ganz kleine Jungfische sind strahlend blau. Das untere Bild zeigt zwei andere Jungfisch-Färbungen. Der Neon-Riffbarsch wird bis zu 15 cm groß. M, K, A.

The systematic position of the second damselfish species is still unclear. Probably it does not belong to the tropical genus Abedefduf that has many species. As is the case of the atlantic damselfish (page 90), territorial males defend an area of slightly overhanging rock-face, which they have carefully cleaned beforehand. Females lay their eggs on this spot and then leave again. The male protects the nest and sometimes even attacks divers. In the top photo one can see the spawn on the left hand side of the picture. As they increase in size the young fish change their colour various times. Very small young fish are a brilliant blue. The bottom photo shows two other colours of young fishes. The bluefin damselfish grows to a size of up to 15 cm. M, K.

Neon-Riffbarsch — Bluefin damselfish — Abudefduf luridus — 93

Lippfische   Wrasses   Labridae

Roter Schweinsfisch   Red hogfish   Pseudolepidaplois scrofa

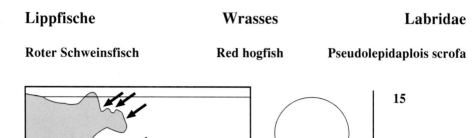

Innerhalb der Lippfische bilden die Schweinsfische eine eigene Unterfamilie. Im subtropischen Ostatlantik gibt es nur die abgebildete Art.
Bei großen Männchen (oberes Bild) ragen die Zähne etwas wie Schweinehauer aus dem Maul hervor. Das untere Bild zeigt ein Weibchen. Das kleine (in 45 m Tiefe aufgenommene) Bild zeigt wahrscheinlich die noch unbeschriebene Jugendfärbung der Art. Bisher ist es aber noch nicht geglückt, so ein Tier zu fangen, um diese Vermutung zu überprüfen. Mit bis zu 65 cm Länge ist der Rote Schweinsfisch die größte Lippfischart im subtropischen Ostatlantik. M, K, A.

Within the wrasses the hogfish form their own subfamily. The species shown is the only one in the subtropical Eastern Atlantic.
Large males' (top photo) teeth project forward out of the mouth somewhat like the tusks of a boar. The bottom photo shows a female. The small photo (taken at a depth of 45 m) shows what is probably the so far undescribed juvenile colour of the species. As of yet no-one has been lucky enough to catch such an animal, to be able to check this guess. The red hogfish, which grows to a length of up to 65 cm, is the biggest wrasse in the subtropical Eastern Atlantic. M, K, A.

Roter Schweinsfisch   Red hogfish   Pseudolepidaplois scrofa   95

Lippfische / Wrasses / Labridae

Meerjunker / **Rainbow wrasse** / *Coris julis*

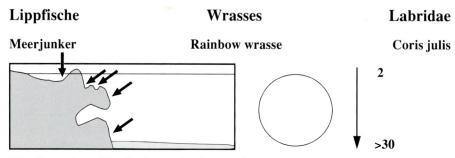

Wie die meisten Lippfische wechselt auch der Meerjunker sein Geschlecht: kleine Tiere sind Weibchen, die jeweils größten Tiere der Population wandeln sich zu Männchen um. Oben rechts: typische Männchen-Färbung, unten rechts: Weibchen, kleines Bild: Jungtiere. Das unten links abgebildete Tier wandelt sich gerade zum Männchen um, ist aber noch recht weibchen-ähnlich. Die Art hat im Atlantik eine etwas andere Färbung als im Mittelmeer, allerdings kommt die "atlantische" Färbung auch an manchen Orten im Mittelmeer vor. M, K, A.

As most of the wrasses, the rainbow wrasse also changes its sex: small animals are female, the largest animals of the population change to males. The photos show the typical colour of males (top photo), females (bottom right) and young animals (small photo); the animal in the bottom left photo is in the process of changing from female to male, but is still quite similar to females. In the Atlantic, the species has a different colour as in the Mediteranean, but the "Atlantic" colour also occurs at some places in the Mediteranean Sea. M, K, A.

| Meerjunker | Rainbow wrasse | Coris julis | 97 |

Lippfische   Wrasses   Labridae

Meerpfau   Turkish wrasse   Thalassoma pavo

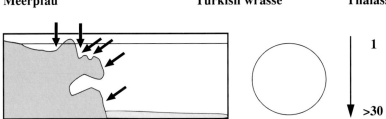

Typisch für Lippfische (und die nahe verwandten Papageifische) ist die Fortbewegung durch Flügelschläge mit den Brustflossen. Die meisten Lippfische haben außerdem ein ziemlich spitzes Maul.

Das obere Bild zeigt die Färbung von Männchen, das untere die Weibchenfarbe. Wie beim Meerjunker (Seite 96) wandeln sich die jeweils größten Weibchen einer Population in Männchen um. Weibchen schwimmen meistens in Gruppen von wenigen Tieren bis zu mehr als hundert Tieren. Beim Ablaichen schwimmt ein dichtes Knäuel von Weibchen mit einem (oder mehreren) Männchen etwa einen Meter nach oben ins freie Wasser, wo die Tiere plötzlich explosionsartig auseinanderstieben und eine Wolke von Eiern und Sperma im Wasser hinterlassen. Die Eier enthalten Öltröpfchen und werden von der Strömung ins Plankton verdriftet. Junge Meerpfauen betätigen sich oft als Putzerfische. Der Meerpfau ernährt sich von kleinen Krebsen und Schnecken. Die Art wird bis zu 25 cm lang, meistens sieht man aber nur 15-20 cm große Tiere. Nachts graben Meerpfauen sich oft in Sand ein. M, K, A.

Typical of wrasses (and the closely related parrotfish) is the way they move which resembles flying with the pectoral fins. Most wrasses also have a rather pointed mouth.

The top photo shows the male colour, the bottom the females colour. As with rainbow wrasses (page 96), the biggest females of the population change to males. Females mostly swim in groups of a few animals up to more than a hundred animals. While spawning a thick clustering of females with one or more males swims up for about a meter into the open water, where suddenly they disperse leaving behind them a cloud of eggs and sperm in the water. The eggs contain droplets of oil and drift away into the plankton. Young turkish wrasse often act as cleaner fish. The turkish wrasse feeds on small crabs and snails. The species grows to a length of up to 25 cm, but mostly one sees animals which are 15-20 cm long. At night most turkish wrasse burrow themselves in sand. M, K, A.

Meerpfau   Turkish wrasse   Thalassoma pavo   **99**

Lippfische   Wrasses   Labridae

Gefleckter Lippfisch   Ballan wrasse   Labrus bergylta

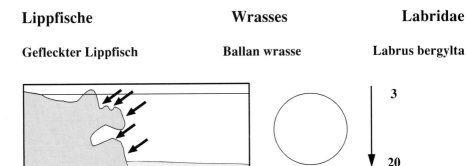

Mit 60 cm Maximallänge gehört diese Art zu den großen Lippfischen. Der Gefleckte Lippfisch variiert in seiner Körperfarbe von dunkelbraun über hellbraun zu grün; manchmal hat er einen weißen Längsstreifen (kleines Bild). Die dicken fleischigen Lippen sind typisch für die Art. Sie kann bis 18 Jahre alt werden. M, K, A.

With a maximum length of 60 cm this species belongs to the big wrasses. The ballan wrasse varies in body colours from dark brown through light brown to grey; sometimes it has a white horizontal stripe (small photo). The thickly fleshed lips are typical for this species. They can reach up to 18 years of age. M, K, A.

Kuckuckslippfisch   Cuckoo wrasse   Labrus bimaculatus

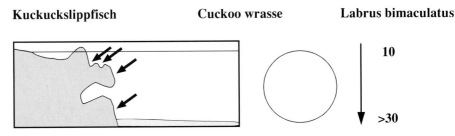

Beim Kuckuckslippfisch sind Männchen und Weibchen sehr verschieden gefärbt. Das große Bild zeigt das farbenprächtige Männchen. Weibchen haben einen roten Körper und drei große rechteckige schwarze Flecken auf dem Rücken (kleines Bild). Die Art wird bis zu 17 Jahre alt und 40 cm groß. M, K, A.

In the cuckoo wrasse's case, the males and females have very different colours. The photo shows a male. Females have a red body and three big rectangular black spots on the back. Cuckoo wrasse can reach 17 years of age and 40 cm in size. M, K, A.

| Gefleckter Lippfisch | Ballan wrasse | Labrus bergylta |
| Kuckuckslippfisch | Cuckoo wrasse | Labrus bimaculatus |

Lippfische   Wrasses   Labridae

Mittelmeer-Lippfisch   Axillary wrasse   Symphodus mediterraneus

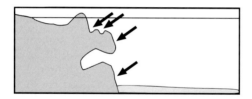 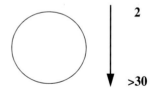

Bei den Lippfische der Gattungen Symphodus und Centrolabrus (nächste Seite) bauen die Männchen zur Laichzeit aus Pflanzenmaterial ein Nest, das einem Vogelnest sehr ähnlich sieht. Territoriale, nestbesitzende Männchen balzen vorbei kommende Weibchen an. Wenn das Weibchen Eier legt, kommen gelegentlich auch nichtterritoriale Männchen angeeilt und sprühen Sperma über das Nest. Das territoriale Männchen, das viel Zeit und Energie in den Bau des Nestes gesteckt hat und anschließend die Eier bis zum Schlüpfen der Larven bewacht, wird so um einen Teil seines Erfolges betrogen.
Zur Laichzeit sind die Männchen viel intensiver gefärbt (oberes Bild) als außerhalb der Laichzeit (unteres Bild). M, K, A.

Males of wrasses of the genus Symphodus and Centrolabrus (next page) build a nest out of plant material in the spawning season, which looks very much like a bird nest. Territorial, nest-owning males court passing females. When the female lays eggs, often non-territorial males come running and spray sperm over the nest. The territorial male who has invested a lot of time and energy in building the nest and in taking care of the eggs until the larvae hatch is thus deprived of part of his gain.
During the spawning season the males have much brighter colours (top photo) than out of the spawning season (bottom photo) M, K, A.

Mittelmeer-Lippfisch   Axillary wrasse   Symphodus mediterraneus   **103**

Lippfische   Wrasses   Labridae

Atlantischer Lippfisch   Atlantic wrasse   Centrolabrus trutta

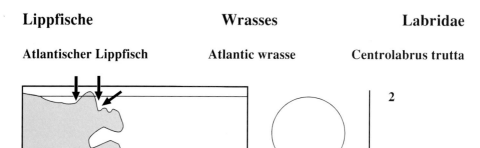

Der Atlantische Lippfisch ist eine der häufigsten Flachwasser-Arten. Zur Laichzeit sind die Männchen auffällig grün gefärbt (oberes Bild), sonst sehen sie so unscheinbar aus wie die Weibchen (kleines Bild). Zum Nestbau verwenden sie nicht nur Pflanzenmaterial sondern auch kleine Steine. M, A.

The atlantic wrasse is one of the most common species in shallow water. During the spawning season, the males are coloured conspicuously (top), outside the spawning season they resemble females (small picture). In nest construction they not only use plant material but also small stones. M, A.

Schermesserfisch   Cleaver wrasse   Xyrichthys novacula

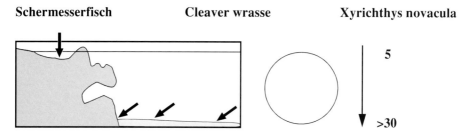

Schermesserfische stehen über Sandboden. Bei Gefahr bohren sie sich blitzschnell kopfvoraus in den Sand ein. Kleine Tiere sind Weibchen; die jeweils größten Tiere wechseln ihr Geschlecht und werden zu Männchen. Weibchen sind blaßgrün oder blaßrosa gefäbt, Männchen deutlich dunkler. Schermesserfische werden bis zu 8 Jahre alt. M, K, A. (Kleines Bild: Jungtier)

Cleaver wrasses hover over sandy bottom. When disturbed they burrow themselves headfirst and with lightning-speed. Small animals are female; the largest animals change sex and turn male. Females are a light green or a light pink, males are darker. Clevaer wrasses reach up to 8 years of age. M, K, A. (Small picture: juvenile)

| Atlantischer Lippfisch | Atlantic wrasse | Centrolabrus trutta |
| Schermesserfisch | Cleaver wrasse | Xyrichthys novacula |

Papageifische   Parrotfish   Scaridae

Papageifisch   **Parrotfish**   **Sparisoma cretense**

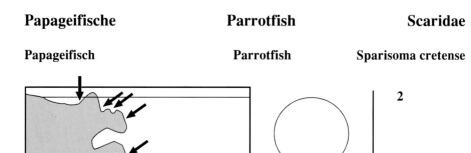

Die Zähne der Papageifische sind zu schnabel-ähnlichen Zahnplatten verschmolzen. Wie die Lippfische, mit denen sie nahe verwandt sind, bewegen sie sich mit "Flügelschlägen" ihrer Brustflossen vorwärts. Sie schaben Algen von Felsen ab oder fressen sogar Kalkalgen und Korallen, die sie mit speziellen Mahlzähnen weit hinten im Schlund zermahlen. Auf der Innenseite der Kiemendeckel liegt eine Drüse, die einen Schleimmantel um schlafende Papageifische bildet. Dieser "Schlafanzug" ist keine Geruchsbarriere, wie man manchmal liest, sondern ein "chemisch neutraler" Mantel der bei Berührung durch Muränen (siehe Seite 32) keinen Zubiß auslöst. Bei den meisten Papageifischen bilden nur Jungtiere eine Schleimhülle zum Schlafen.
In der Familie Papageifische gibt es etwa 70 Arten. Bei tropischen Arten sind die Männchen auffallend bunt gefärbt, die Weibchen eher unscheinbar braun, grün, oder grau. Der Europäische Papageifisch ist anscheinend die einzige Art, bei der es umgekehrt ist: die Männchen sind grau (unteres Bild), die Weibchen auffallend rot und gelb gefärbt (oberes Bild). Jungfische sind gelb (kleines Bild). M, K, A.

The teeth of parrotfishes are fused to form beak-like plates. Like the wrasses, with whom they are closely related, their movements resemble flying with the pectoral fins. They scrape algae from rocks or even feed on cacareous algae and coral, which they grind to small pieces with the help of special pharyngeal teeth. A gland on the inner side of the operculum produces a slime envelope around sleeping parrot fishes. This pyjama is not a barrier for the smell of the animals, as one can sometimes read, but a "chemically neutral" coat that does not elicit the morays' bite upon contact (see page 32). In most parrot fish species, only the young produce a slime envelope when sleeping.
There are about 70 pecies in the family parrot fishes. In tropical species, the male is conspicuously couloured, whereas females are a drab brown, green, or grey. The european parrotfish apparently is the only species where the opposite is true: males are grey (lower picture) and females are a conspicuous red and yellow (upper picture). Juveniles are yellow (small picture). M, K, A.

| Papageifisch | Parrotfish | Sparisoma cretense | 107 |

Petermännchen	**Weevers**	**Trachinidae**
Gestreiftes Petermännchen	Streaked weever	Trachinus radiatus
Großes Petermännchen	Greater weever	Trachinus draco

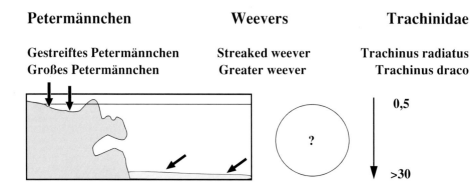

Petermännchen liegen meistens halb vergraben in Sandboden, wo sie nach anderen Fischen lauern. Die erste Rückenflosse, die sie bei Gefahr aufstellen, hat kräftige Stachelstrahlen mit Giftdrüsen an der Basis.

Da Petermännchen an windgeschützten Küsten auch im ganz flachem Wasser liegen können, sind vor allem Badende gefährdet, die ohne Schuhe ins Wasser gehen. Stichverletzungen sind in der Regel nicht lebensgefährlich, aber geradezu unbeschreiblich schmerzhaft. Erste Hilfe besteht in Einreiben mit Kaliumpermanganat (das aber in den seltensten Fällen zur Hand ist) und in möglichst heißen Bädern der verletzten Stelle.

Das Gestreifte Petermännchen wird bis zu 30 cm groß, das Große Petermännchen bis 40 cm. Gestreiftes Petermännchen: K. Großes Petermännchen M, K.

Weevers usually are half burried in sandy bottom, where they are lying in wait for small fish. The first dorsal fin, erected when the animal feels threatened, consists of strong spiny rays and has poison glands at its base. As weevers can occur even in very shallow water in wave-protected bays, its is mainly people entering water without shoes that are in danger of being stung and poisoned. Normally, the sting is not dangerous to life. It is, however, painful to an extreme degree. First aid consist in rubbing the wound with potassium permanganate (rarely there when one needs it) and in bathing the wound in water as hot as possible.

The streaked weever reaches 30 cm in lenght, the greater weever 40 cm. Streaked weever K. Greater weever M, K.

| Gestreiftes Petermännchen | Streaked weever | Trachinus radiatus |
| Großes Petermännchen | Greater weever | Trachinus draco |

Himmelsgucker   Stargazers   Uranoscopidae

Himmelsgucker   Stargazer   Uranoscopus scaber

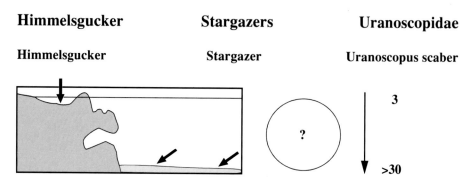

Himmelsgucker sind oft so tief im Sand vergraben, daß die meisten Taucher sie nicht sehen: nur die Augen und die Mundspalte liegen frei. Sie haben zwar keine Giftstacheln in der Rückenflosse, dafür aber am Kiemendeckel. Mit einem beweglichen Hautlappen am Unterkiefer locken sie kleine Fische in die Reichweite ihres großen Maules. Diesen können sie auch benutzen, um sich den Kopf abzuwischen. M, K.

Stargazers are often burried in the sand so deeply that most divers do not see them: only the eyes and the mouth are uncovered. Stargazers do not have poison spines in the dorsal fin, but they do have poison spines on the gill covers. With a movable skin flap on the lower lip they attract small fish into the reach of their large mouth. They can also use this skin flap to wipe their head. M, K.

Schiffshalter   Sharksuckers   Echeneididae

Schiffshalter   Common remora   Remora remora

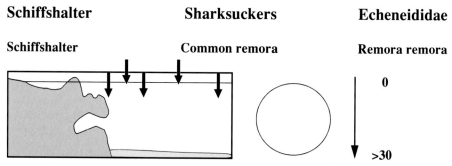

Die erste Rückenflosse der Schiffshalter ist zu einem Saugorgan umgewandelt, mit dem sie sich an Mantas (siehe auch Seiten 19 und 21), Haie, Schwertfische, Wale und gelegentlich auch Schiffe anhängen. Jungtiere sind Putzerfische für ihre Transporteure. Wenn die Schiffshalter größer werden, fressen sie kleine Fische. Die Art wird mindestens 60 cm lang. M, K, A.

The first dorsal fin of sharksuckers is modified to form a suction disk, by which they cling to mantas (see pages 19 and 21), sharks, swordfish, whales, and even to ships. Young animals act as cleaner fish for their carriers. When grown to a larger size, sharksuckers feed on small fish. The common remora reaches at least 60 cm length. M, K, A.

Himmelsgucker — Stargazer — Uranoscopus scaber

Schiffshalter — Common remora — Remora remora

Makrelen und Tune   Mackerels and Tunas   Scombridae

Bonito   **Atlantic bonito**   **Sarda sarda**

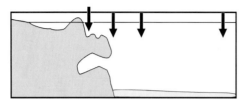 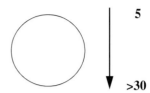

Makrelen und Tune sind Raubfische des offenen Meeres. Taucher werden sie deshalb nur selten sehen. Der Körper ist torpedoförmig und die Schwanzflosse tief gegabelt. Zwischen der Rückenflosse (die meistens in eine Grube auf dem Rücken versenkt werden kann) und der Schwanzflosse steht eine Reihe von Flösselchen.

Am ehesten sieht man als Taucher, vor allem bei den Azoren, den Bonito. Es ist ein beeindruckendes Erlebnis, wenn aus dem offenen Meer eine Gruppe von Bonitos auf den Taucher zubraust, ihn einmal umkreist und wieder ins Blaue entschwindet. Der Bonito wird bis zu 1m lang und 5 kg schwer. M, K, A.

An manchen Tauchbasen hat sich die Unsitte eingebürgert, Bernsteinmakrelen (Seite 84) Thunfische zu nennen; das ist schlicht falsch.

Mackerels and tuna are predators of the open seas. Divers therefor see them only rarely. The body is torpedo-shaped and the caudal fin is deeply forked. Between the dorsal fin (which in many species can be folded into a groove on the back) and the tail fin there is a row of small finlets.

As a diver one is most likely to see the atlantic bonito, in particular at the Azores. It is a very impresive experience when a group of atlantic bonitos races towards the diver, coming from the open sea, circles once around him, and disappears again into the blue. The atlantic bonito reaches up to 1m length and 5 kg weight. M, K, A.

At some SCUBA diving bases, the bad habit of calling amberjacks (page 84) tunas has established itself. This is simply wrong.

Bonito   Atlantic Bonito   Sarda sarda ▶

Dreiflosser Triplefin Blennies Tripterygiidae

Gelber Dreiflosser Yellow triplefin Tripterygion delaisi

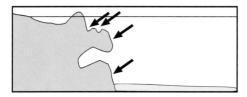
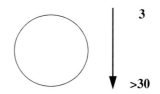

Die Dreiflosser sind nahe mit den Blenniiden (Seite 116) verwandt. Im Gegensatz zu den schuppenlosen Blenniiden haben sie aber Schuppen. Drei Rückenflossen (eine ganz kurze und zwei lange) sind das namensgebende Merkmal. Bei Madeira, den Azoren und den Kanaren gibt es nur den Gelben Dreiflosser, der auch im Mittelmeer lebt.
Zur Laichzeit haben territorial Männchen einen leuchtend gelben Körper und einen schwarzen Kopf. Weibchen und nicht-territoriale Männchen sind unscheinbar graubraun gefärbt. Das Bild zeigt ein ablaichendes Pärchen. Nachdem es seine Eier im Territorium des Männchens abgelegt hat, geht das Weibchen wieder weg. Das Männchen pflegt (putzt) und verteidigt die Eier bis zum Schlüpfen der Larven. Die Larven treiben etwa zwei Monate lang im Plankton, ehe sie irgendwo an einer Felsküste zum Bodenleben übergehen.
Der Gelbe Dreiflosser wird bis zu 7 cm groß und nur zweieinhalb Jahre alt.
M, K, A.

Triplefin blennies are closely related to blennies (page 116). In contrast to blennies, which lack scales, they do have scales. They own their name to the presence of three dorsal fins, a shirt one and two long ones. At Madeira, the Canaries, and the Azores, only the yellow triplefin occurs, which also lives in the Mediterranean Sea.
During the spawning season, territorial males have a brilliantly yellow body and a black head. Females and non-territorial males are a drab grey. The photo shows a spawning pair. After depositing the eggs in the territory of a male, the female leaves. It is the male that cleans and defends the eggs until the larvae hatch. The larve drift in the plancton for about two months, until they settle somewhere at a rocky shore. The yellow triplefin grows to 7 cm lenght and reaches an age of not more than two and a half years. M, K, A.

Blenniiden Blennies Blenniidae

Roter Blenni Red blenny Parablennius ruber

Blennis sind kleine, bodenlebende Arten, die sich vor allem durch große Neugier auszeichnen. In Anpassung an das Bodenleben sind die Augen weit nach vorne oben gerückt. Männchen verteidigen eine kleine Höhle oder Spalte als Territorium und balzen vorbeikommende Weibchen durch heftiges Kopfnicken oder andere auffallende Bewegungen an. Rechts: Männchen im leeren Gehäuse einer großen Seepocke (Megabalanus tintinabulum); unten: etwas blasser gefärbtes Weibchen. M, A.

Blennies are small inquisitive bottom-dwelling species. As an adaptation to life on the sea floor their eyes are located well forward at the top of their heads. Males defend small holes or cracks as territories and court passing females by vigorous nodding movements of the head and by other movements capturing attention. Right: male red blenny in an empty shell of a giant barnacle (Megabalanus tintinabulum), below: the lighter coloured female. M, A.

Blenniiden   Blennies   Blenniidae

Grauer Blenni   Grey blenny   Lipophrys trigloides

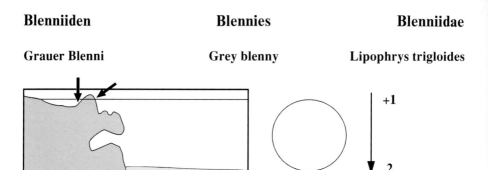

Der Graue Blenni gehört zu den wenigen Fischarten, die regelmäßig das Wasser verlassen. Tagsüber findet man sie in der Brandungszone, nachts schlafen manche (alle ?) Tiere dieser Art etwas oberhalb der Wasserlinie, wo sie gerade noch ab und zu von Wellen befeuchtet werden. M, K, A.

The grey blenny is one of the few species of fish that regularly leave the water. During the day it lives on rocks in the surf zone, at night some (all ?) of them sleep above the waterline, at a level where an occasional wave every now and then keeps them wet. M, K, A.

Brauner Blenni   Brown blenny   Parablennius incognitus

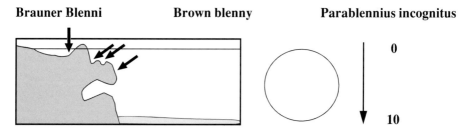

Der Braune Blenni ist mit Abstand die häufigste Blenniiden-Art im Mittelmeer. Bei Madeira, den Kanaren und den Azoren ist er eher selten. Die Tentakel über den Augen sind bei den Männchen viel länger als bei Weibchen. Obwohl er nur bis zu 6 cm groß wird, kann der Braune Blenni 7 Jahre alt werden. M, K, A.

The brown blenny is by far the most common blenny species in the Mediterranean sea. At Madeira, the Canary islands, and the Azores it is not common. The tentacles above the eyes are much longer in males than in females. Despite reaching a length of only 6 cm, the brown blenny can attain an age of up to 7 years. M, K, A.

| Grauer Blenni | Grey blenny | Lipophrys trigloides |
| Brauner Blenni | Brown blenny | Parablennius incognitus |

Blenniiden	**Blennies**	**Blenniidae**
Rotlippenblenni	Redlip blenny	Ophioblennius atlanticus
Seeschmetterling	Butterfly blenny	Blennius ocellaris

Mit bis zu 25cm Länge ist der Rotlippenblenni die größte Blenniiden Art im Atlantik. Im Bereich von 1 bis 12 m ist er recht häufig. Im Gegensatz zu den drei vorigen Arten ist er ein Pflanzenfresser. Das untere Bild zeigt die Nachtfärbung. M, K, A.

Der Seeschmetterling hält den Tiefenrekord unter den ostatlantischen Blenniden: er wurde noch in mehr als 400 m Tiefe gefangen und ist oberhalb von 30 m sehr selten zu sehen. Er wird bis zu 12 cm groß. A.

With up to 25 cm length the redlip blenny is the largest blenny species in the Atlantic. At a depth of one to twelve meters it is quite common. In contrast to the three previous species, the redlip blenny eats only plants. The lower photo shows the colour pattern of sleeping animals. M, K, A.

The butterfly blenny holds the depth record among the Eastern Atlantic blennies: it has been caught at depths of more than 400 m and is only rarely encountered in water shallower than 30 m. The butterfly blenny grows to 12 cm length. A.

| Seeschmetterling | Butterfly blenny | Blennius ocellaris |

| Rotlippenblenni | Redlip blenny | Ophioblennius atlanticus | 121 |

Beschuppte Blenniiden   Scaled Blennies   Labrisomidae

Schopfblenni   Hairy blenny   Labrisomus nuchipinnis

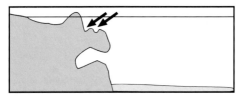 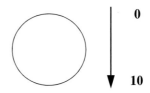

0

10

Die Beschuppten Blenniiden sind eine tropische Fischgruppe. Im subtropischen Ostatlantik ist der Schopfblenni die einzige Art; bei Madeira erreicht sie ihre nördliche Verbreitunggrenze. Auf dem Nacken, vor der Rückenflosse steht eine Reihe kurzer, dünner, haarförmiger Tentakel. Der Schopfblenni ist ein Raubfisch, der anderen kleinen Fischen auflauert. Er erreicht eine Größe von bis zu 21cm cm und kann seine Farbe der der Umgebung anpassen. M, K.

The scaled blennies are a tropical group of fish. In the subtropical Eastern Atlantic the hairy blenny is the only species. At Madeira it reaches its northern limit of distribution. On the nape, in front of the dorsal fin, grows a row of short, thin, hair-like tentacles. The hairy blenny is a predator, lying in wait for small fish. It reaches a size of up to 21 cm and can adapt the brightness of its colour to that of the surrounding. M, K.

Schopfblenni   Hairy blenny   Labrisomus nuchipinnis▶

Grundeln   Gobies   Gobiidae

Leopardengrundel   **Leopard spotted goby**   **Thorogobius epphipiatus**

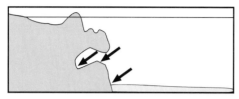 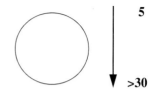

Die Grundeln werden häufig mit den Blenniiden verwechselt. Bei den Grundeln sind aber die Bauchflossen zu einem Saugnapf verschmolzen, während sie bei den Blenniiden zwei kleine "Füße" bilden, die weit vorne an der Kehle sitzen. Die Leopardengrundel lebt auf Sand- und Schlammboden in Höhlen und am Fuß von Felsüberhängen. M, K, A.

Gobies are frequently confused with blennies, but in the gobies the pelvic fins are united to form a suction disk, whereas in the blennies the pelvic fins are formed like two small "legs" and are situated far forward on the throat. The leopard spotted goby lives on sandy and muddy bottoms in caves and at the foot of overhangs. M, K, A.

Felsgrundel   **Rock goby**   **Gobius paganellus**

Mit mehr als tausendfünfhundert Arten sind die Grundeln die größte Fischfamilie. Wie der Name sagt lebt die Felsgrundel an Felsküsten. Meistens ist sie unter Steinen versteckt. Beide hier abgebildeten Arten werden etwa 12 cm groß und bis zu 9 Jahre alt. M, K, A.

Containing more than 1.500 species, the gobies are the largest family of marine fish. As the name indicates, the rock goby lives at rocky shores. Usually it hides below stones. Both species shown here grow to about 12 cm length and up to 9 years of age. M, K, A.

| Leopardengrundel | Leopard spotted goby | Thorogobius epphipiatus |
| Felsgrundel | Rock goby | Gobius paganellus |

Knurrhähne   Gurnards   Triglidae

Gestreifter Knurrhahn   Streaked gurnard   Trigloporus lastoviza

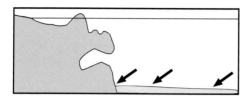 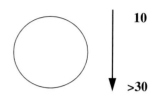

Die ersten zwei bis drei Strahlen der Brustflosen der Knurrhähne sind wie Finger frei beweglich. Damit fühlen sie auf Sand und Schlammboden nach Nahrung. Auf den Spitzen der Flossenstrahlen sitzen Geschmacksknospen, so daß die Knurrhähne auch gleich schmecken, was sie berührt haben. Knurrhähne heißen Knurrhähne, weil sie knurrende Laute ausstoßen können.

Die häufigste Knurrhahn-Art im subtropischen Ostatlantik ist der Gestreifte Knurrhahn. Bei Bedrohung breitet er seine großen blau-gesäumten Brustflossen aus (oberes Bild). Er wird bis 40 cm lang. M, K, A.

The first two to three rays of the pectoral fins of gurnards are movable like fingers. Using them, the gurnards feel for food in sand and mud. There are taste buds on the tips of these fin rays so that the gurnards can actually taste what they have touched. The German name "Knurrhahn" comes from the animals' ability to emit grunting noises.

The streaked gurnard is the most common gurnard species in the Eastern Atlantic. When feeling threatened it unfolds its large blue-rimmed pectoral fins (top). It reaches 40 cm in size. M, K, A.

| Gestreifter Knurrhahn | Streaked gurnard | Trigloporus lastoviza | 127 |

Skorpionsfische   Scorpionfish   Scorpaenidae

Skorpionsfische verdanken ihren Namen den vielen giftigen Stacheln und Dornen, die sie auf dem Körper tragen. Meistens liegen sie auf Felsgrund, wo sie auf kleine Fische und Krebse lauern.

The name scorpionfish is due to the presence of many poisonous spines on the body of these fish. Usually, they rest on rocky bottom, lying in wait for small fish.

Großer Roter Drachenkopf   Red scorpionfish   Scorpaena scrofa

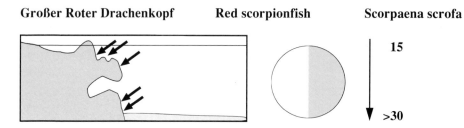

Der Große Rote Drachenkopf wird bis 65 cm lang. Im flachen Wasser sieht man vor allem Jungtiere bis etwa 20 oder 30 cm Länge; die großen Exemplare leben in Tiefen bis zu 300 m. M, K, A.

The red scorpionfish reaches 65 cm in length. In shallow water one usually sees young animals of up to 20 or 30 cm. The large individuals live at depths down to 300 m. M, K, A.

Brauner Drachenkopf   Brown scorpionfish   Scorpaena porcus

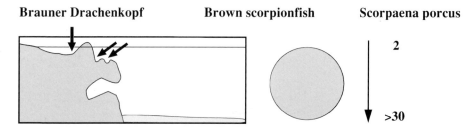

Der Braune Drachenkopf wird bis 25 cm lang, am häufigsten sieht man aber Tiere von etwa 10 cm Länge. Er legt sich meist dicht neben ein Pflanzenbüschel und wird wegen seiner perfekten Tarnung fast immer übersehen. M, K, A.

The brown scorpionfish grows to 25 cm in size, but commonly one sees animals of only about 10 cm. The brown scorpionfish frequently rests next to clumps of plants and due to its perfect camouflage is easily overlooked. M, K, A.

| Großer Roter Drachenkopf | Red scorpionfish | Scorpaena scrofa |
| Brauner Drachenkopf | Brown scorpionfish | Scorpaena porcus |

Skorpionsfische   Scorpionfish   Scorpaenidae

Madeira-Drachenkopf   **Madeira scorpionfish**   **Scorpaena maderensis**

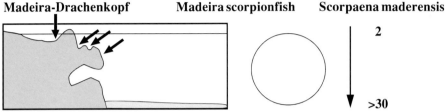

2

\>30

Die Art, die nicht nur bei Madeira sondern auch bei den Azoren und an der ostatlantischen Küste bis Senegal lebt, ist an ihrer typisch gebänderten Zeichnung zu erkennen; die Grundfarbe kann dabei von rot über braun zu grau variieren. Zur Bestimmung von Drachenköpfen verwenden Fischsystematiker auch die Zahl und Anordnung der Dornen am Kopf. M, K, A.

The madeira scorpionfish, which lives not only at Madeira but also at the Azores and at the Eastern Atlantic coasts south to Senegal, can be recognized by the species-typical banded colour pattern; the background colour of the body can vary from grey to brown to red. Fish systematicians also use the number and arangement of spines on the head to identify scorpionfish. M, K, A.

Butte   Left-eye Flounders   Bothidae

Weitaugenbutt   **Wide-eyed flounder**   **Bothus podas**

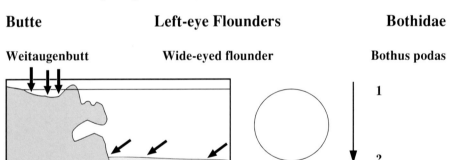

1

?

Butte sind eine von 6 Plattfisch-Familien. Sie haben die Augen auf der linken Körperseite. Die Männchen dieser Art (Foto) haben einen deutlich größeren Abstand zwischen den Augen als die Weibchen. Niemand weiß, warum. Als "Abstauber", die nach aufgescheuchten Tieren schnappen, schwimmen Weitaugenbutte manchmal hinter anderen Arten her, z.B. großen Seesternen oder Meerbarben (S. 78). M, K, A.

Left-eyed flounders are one of six flatfish families. They have their eyes on the left side of the body. In males of the wide-eyed flounder (photo) the distance between the eyes is much larger than in females. Nobody knows, why. As "scroungers", that snap at animals stirred up, Wide-eyed flounders sometimes follow other animals such as large starfish or striped mullets (page 78). M, K, A.

| Madeira-Drachenkopf | Madeira scorpionfish | Scorpaena maderensis |
| Weitaugenbutt *Weibchen* | Wide-eyed flounder | Bothus podas |

Seezungen   Soles   Soleidae

Augenfleck-Seezunge   **Eyed sole**   **Microchirus ocellatus**

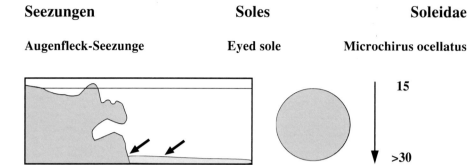

Im Gegensatz zu den Hundszungen (siehe unten) haben die Seezungen die Augen auf der rechten Körperseite. In der Körperform sind sie den Hundszungen sehr ähnlich. Nur nachts und recht selten sieht man die prächtig gefärbte Augenfleck-Seezunge. Sie wird bis 20 cm groß. M, K.

In contrast to tonguesoles (see below), soles have their eyes on the right side of the body. Their body shape resembles that of the tonguesoles. It is only at night and quite rarely that one encounters an eyed sole. It can reach a size of up to 20 cm. M, K.

Hundszungen   Tonguesoles   Cynoglossidae

Gefleckte Hundszunge   **Spotted tonguesole**   **Symphurus reticulatus**

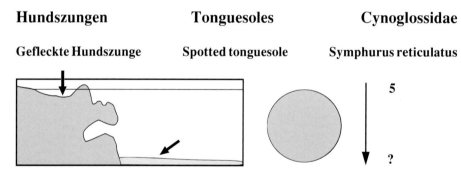

Die Hundszungen sehen den Seezungen sehr ähnlich, aber ihre Augen liegen auf der anderen Seite des Körpers, auf der linken. Die abgebildete Art ist an ihren hellen X- und Y-förmigen Streifen auf dem Körper zu erkennen. Sie ist erst 1990 zum erstenmal beschrieben worden und wird anscheinend nur 6 cm groß. M.

Tonguesoles greatly resemble soles (see above) but they have their eyes just on the other side of the body, namely the left. The spotted tonguesole can be recognized by the Y- and X-shaped stripes on the body. The species has only been described in 1990 and apparently reaches only 6 cm in length. M.

Augenfleck-Seezunge	Eyed sole	Microchirus ocellatus
Gefleckte Hundszunge	Spotted tonguesole	Symphurus reticulatus

Drückerfische	Triggerfish	Balistidae
Grauer Drückerfish	Gray triggerfish	Balistes carolinensis

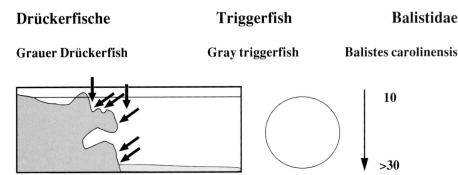

10

>30

Die erste Rückenflosse der Drückerfische und Feilenfische hat einen raffinierten Arretierungsmechanismus: ein kleiner Fortsatz am 2. Flossenstrahl rastet in eine Grube am ersten Flossenstrahl ein. Der besonders kräftige erste Flossenstrahl ist dadurch fest verankert, und für viele Raubfische ist der Drückerfisch dann viel zu schwierig zu Fressen. M, K, A.

The first dorsal fin of triggerfish and filefish has an ingeneous locking mechanisms: a small projection of the second fin ray clicks into a groove in the first fin ray. The particularly stout first dorsal fin ray then is securely fastened in an upright position and for many predatory fish the triggerfish thus is far too unwieldy to eat. M, K, A.

Feilenfische	Filefish	Monacanthidae
Brauner Feilenfisch	Brown filefish	Stephanolepis hispidus

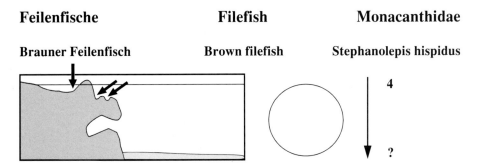

4

?

Feilenfische haben kleine Schuppen mit winzigen Dornen drauf: ihre Haut fühlt sich an wie Sandpapier. Die Bauchflossen sind noch weiter reduziert als bei den Drückerfischen. Wie die Drückerfische schwimmen sie mit rudernden Bewegungen der Rücken- und Afterflossen. Die abgebildete Art (die einzige im subtropischen Ostatlantik) wird nur 15 cm groß. M, K, A.

Filefish have small scales with tiny spines on them: their skin feels like sand paper. The pelvic fins are even further reduced than in the triggerfish. Like the triggerfish, they swimm with propelling movements of the dorsal and anal fins. The species shown (the only one in the subtropical Eastern Atlantic) reaches up to 15 cm in length. M, K, A.

| Grauer Drückerfisch | Gray triggerfish | Balistes carolinensis |
| Brauner Feilenfisch | Brown filefish | Stephanolepis hispidus |

Kugelfische   Pufferfish   Tetraodontidae

Spitzkopf-Kugelfish   **Sharpnose puffer**   **Canthigaster rostrata**

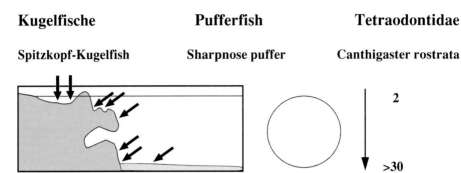

Der wissenschaftliche Name der Kugelfische "Tetraodontidae" heißt "Vierzähner": Die Zähne im Ober- und Unterkiefer sind zu je zwei großen Zähnen verschmolzen. Bei Gefahr können sich die Kugelfische aufblasen, indem sie Wasser verschlucken (Bild unten rechts).
Der Spitzkopf-Kugelfisch wird bis zu 10 cm groß und lebt auf beiden Seiten des Atlantiks. Weibchen verteidigen Territorien gegen andere Weibchen und gegen kleine Männchen. Große Männchen verteidigen ein Gebiet, das die Territorien mehrerer Weibchen enthält. Zur Laichzeit baut das Weibchen ein kleines Nest aus Algen. Dort werden die Eier abgelegt, aber dann nicht weiter bewacht. Wie viele andere Jungfische (siehe auch Seite 85 unten) verstecken sich auch die jungen Kugelfische gerne zwischen Seeigelstacheln (Bild unten links). M, K.

The scientific name "Tetraodontidae" for the puffer fish means "having four teeth": the teeth are fused into two large teeth in the upper and in the lower yaw. When feeling threatened pufferfish can inflate themselves by swallowing water (bottom right).
The sharpnose puffer reaches a size of up to 10 cm and lives on both sides of the Atlantic. Females defend territories against other females and against small males. Large males defend an area that contains the territories of several females. During the spawning season the female build a nest of small algae, into which the eggs are deposited. The spawn is not guarded afterwards. Like many other juvenile fish (see for instance page 85 below) juvenile pufferfish like to hide between the spines of sea urchins (bottom left). M, K.

Spitzkopf-Kugelfish		Sharpnose puffer		Canthigaster rostrata	137

Kugelfische Pufferfish Tetraodontidae

Brauner Kugelfisch **Brown puffer** **Sphoeroides marmoratus**

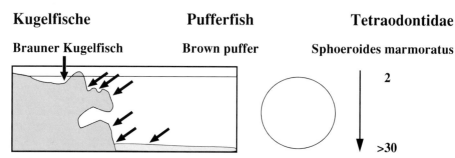

Außer durch ihre Fähigkeit, sich aufzublasen, sind Kugelfische auch noch durch ein starkes Gift, das Tetrodotoxin, vor Raubfeinden geschützt. Es wird in den Eingeweiden, vor allem der Leber, gespeichert. Im westl. Atlantik lebt die sehr ähnliche und ganz nahe verwandte Art S. spengleri, eines von vielen Beispielen für sogenannte "Schwesterarten" auf den beiden Seiten des Atlantiks. Der Braune Kugelfisch wird bis 20 cm groß, aber Exemplare größer als 10 cm sieht man nur selten. M, K, A.

Not only because of their ability to inflate themselves but also because they are highly poisonous, pufferfish are protected against most predators. The poison, called Tetrodotoxin, is stored in the intestines, mainly the liver. In the western Atlantic a very similar and closely related species occurs, Sphoeroides spengleri; this is one of many examples of so-called "sister species" occurring on both sides of the Atlantic. The brown puffer reaches up to 20 cm in length but one rarely sees animals larger than 10 cm. M, K, A.

Igelfische Porcupinefish Diodontidae

Igelfisch **Porcupinefish** **Diodon hystrix**

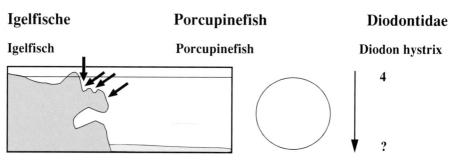

Innerhalb der Igelfische kann man zwei Gruppen unterscheiden: manche Arten (z.B. Gattung Diodon) haben lange Dornen, die sich nur aufrichten, wenn der Fisch sich wie ein Kugelfisch aufbläst; andere Arten (z.B. Gattung Chilomycterus) haben kurze Dornen, die in aufgerichteter Stellung fixiert sind. Diodon hystrix hat eine weltweite tropische und subtropische Verbreitung und wird bis zu 90 cm groß. M, K, A.

Within the porcupinefish two groups can be told apart: some species (e.g. genus Diodon) have long spines that are erected only when the animal inflates itself, other species (e.g. genus Chilomycterus) have short spines that are permanently fixed in an upright position. Diodon hystrix has a worldwide subtropical and tropical distribution and reaches up to 90 cm in length. M, K, A.

| Brauner Kugelfisch | Brown puffer | Sphoeroides marmoratus |
| Igelfisch | Porcupinefish | Diodon hystrix |

Ansauger	Clingfish	Gobiesocidae
Zweifleck-Ansauger Purpur-Ansauger	Twospot clingfish Purple clingfish	Diplecogaster bimaculata Lepadogaster candollei

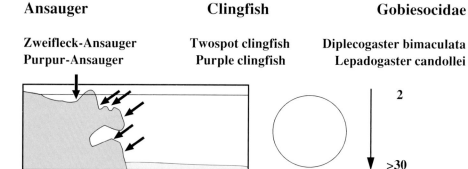

Nicht nur unter Steinen und in Spalten, sondern häufig auch unter Seeigeln sitzen die kleinen Ansauger. An ihrem hechtartig verbreitertem Maul sind sie leicht zu erkennen. Dank ihres großen Mauls können sie für ihre eigene Körperlänge ungewöhnlich große Beute verschlingen. Die Bauchflossen der Ansauger sind zu einem Saugnapf umgewandelt, mit dem sie sich auch bei starker Brandung an der Stelle halten können. Ihre Färbung können die Ansauger weitgehend der des Untergrundes anpassen. Das Männchen bewacht die vom Weibchen in eine kleine Höhle (z.B. eine leere Muschelschale) abgelegten Eier. Der Zweifleck-Ansauger wird nur 3 cm groß, der Purpur-Ansauger immerhin 8 cm. Zweifleck-Ansauger M, K, A. Purpur-Ansauger M, K.

The small clingfish hide not only below stones and in cracks but frequently also below sea urchins. They can be recognized by their wide mouths resembling that of pikes. Due to the enormous gape of their mouths they can swallow prey amazingly large when one considers their own small size. The pelic fins are fused to form a suction disk that allows them to hold their position even in strong surf. Clingfish can adapt the brightnes of their colour pattern to that of their surrounding. It is the male that guards the eggs which the female has deposited into a small cavity, such as an empty mussel shell. The twospot clingfish reaches only 3 cm in size, the purple clingfish grows to 8 cm. Twospot clingfish M, K, A. Purple clingfish M, K.

| Zweifleck-Ansauger | Twospot clingfish | Diplecogaster bimaculata |
| Purpur-Ansauger | Purple clingfish | Lepadogaster candollei |

| **Eingeweidefische** | **Pearlfish** | **Carapidae** |

| **Eingeweidefisch** | **Pearlfish** | **Carapus acus** |

Der Eingeweidefisch lebt als Parasit im Inneren von Seegurken, wo er gelegentlich an den Körpergeweben der Seegurke frißt. Nachts kommt er aber auch aus seiner Seegurke heraus und geht auf die Jagd. Am Morgen fädelt er sich dann wieder Schwanz voraus in die Kloakenöffnung der Seegurke ein. Er wird bis zu 20 cm lang. M, K.

The pearlfish lives as a parasite in the body of sea cucumbers. He sometimes feeds on the intestines of the sea cucumber. But at night the pearlfish can also leave the sea cucumber and go hunting. At dawn it enters again a sea cucumber, tail first and by the cloacal opening of the sea cucumber. It grows to a size of 20 cm. M, K.

| Eingeweidefisch | Pearlfish | Carapus acus ▶ |

Krötenfische Frogfishes Antennariidae

Krötenfisch Frogfish Antennarius nummifer

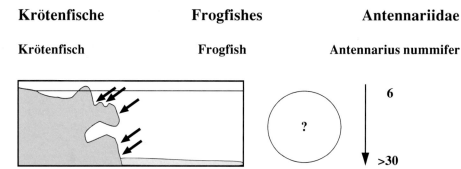

Einen Krötenfisch zu sehen, ist ein seltenes Ereignis. Die Tiere liegen bewegungslos auf Felsboden oder an der Grenze von Sand zu Fels und drücken sich meistens auch noch mit dem Körper an den Felsen. Aufgrund der Regungslosigkeit, der bizarren Gestalt und der recht geringen Körpergröße (bis 9 cm) werden die wenigen Krötenfische, die es gibt, regelmäßig übersehen. Die Brustflossen sind zu kräftigen Armen umgestaltet, mit denen sich die Tiere an Felsvorsprünge klammern können. Mit einer kleinen Angel, dem umgebildeten ersten Strahl der Rückenflosse, und dem daranhängenden beweglichen Hautlappen lockt sich der Krötenfisch kleine Fische und Garnelen vors Maul. Wenn sie nahe genug sind, saugt er sie blitzschnell ein, in dem er sein riesiges Maul weit aufreist. Diese Bewegung ist so schnell, daß sie das menschliche Auge gar nicht wahrnehmen kann; erst durch Zeitlupenaufnahmen konnte man sie analysieren. M, K.

It is a rare experience to see a frogfish. The animals lie motionless on rocky bottom or where rocky bottom meets sandy bottom and press their body against the substrate. Because they do not move, because of their odd shape, and because of their small size (up to 9 cm) the few frogfish in an area are almost always overlooked. The pectoral fins are modified into strong arms, by which the animals cling to ledges. Frogfish attract small fish and shrimps into the reach of their mouths with the help of a small fishing rod that is the modified first ray of the dorsal fin and bears a small skin flap at its end. When the prey has come close enough the frogfish sucks it up by suddenly opening its large mouth. This movement is so fast the the human eye cannot perceive it; it could be analyzed only using slow motion photography. M, K.

Krötenfisch — Frogfish — Antennarius nummifer — **145**

Namen der Arten auf Madeira, den Azoren und den Kanaren
Madeiran, Azorean, and Canarian names of the species

	MADEIRA	AZORES	CANARIES	p
Abudefduf luridus	Castanheta preta	Castanheta preta	Fula negra	92
Antennarius nummifer				142
Anthias anthias	Imperador	Folião	Fula amarilla	62
Apogon imberbis	Alfonsinho da costa		Alfonsito	62
Ariosoma balearicum	Congro das Baleares			38
Atherina presbyter	Guelro		Guelde	46
Aulostomus strigosus	Trombeta		Peje trompeta	46
Balistes carolinensis	Peixe porco	Peixe porco	Gallo	134
Belone belone	Agulinha	Peixe agulha	Aguja	42
Boops boops	Boga	Boga	Boga	70
Bothus podas	Solinha	Solha	Tapaculo	130
Canthigaster rostrata	Porquinho		Gallinita	136
Capros aper	Tem-te-em-pé	Peixe pau		54
Carapus birpex	Peixe cobrelo			142
Centrolabrus trutta	Truta verde	Bodião verde	Romero	104
Chromis limbata	Castanheta baia	Castanhete amarela	Fula	90
Conger conger	Congro	Congro	Congrio	38
Coris julis	Peixe rei	Peixe rei	Carajillo real	96
Dasyatis pastinaca	Ratão	Ratão	Chucho	22
Dentex gibbosus	Pargo de bandeira		Pargo	78
Diodon hystrix	Sapo de espinhos			138
Diplodus cervinus	Sargo veado		Sargo breado	68
Diplodus sargus	Sargo	Sargo	Sargo	66
Diplodus vulgaris	Seifia		Seifía	66
Enchelycore anatina	Moreia serpente	Vibora	Bogavante	34
Epinephelus marginatus	Mero	Mero	Mero	58
Gaidropsarus guttatus	Abrótea da poça	Viuva		44
Gobius paganellus	Velha	Bochecha		124
Gymnothorax unicolor	Moreão	Moreão	Murión	34
Gymnura altavela	Uge-manta		Mariposa	24
Hemirhamphus balao			Aguja	42
Heteroconger longissimus	Enguia de jardim		Anguila jardinera	40
Heteropriacanthus cruentatus	Vaso		Catalufa	64
Hippocampus ramulosus	Cavalo marinho	Cavalo marinho	Caballito de mar	48
Kyphosus sectatrix	Preguiçosa	Patruça	Chopón	78
Labrisomus nuchipinnis			Bullón	122

	MADEIRA	AZORES	CANARIES	p
Labrus bergylta	Truta vermelha	Bodiao vermelho	Romero capitán	100
Labrus bimaculatus	Trombetao	Peixe rei do alto		100
Lepadogaster candollei	Sugador		Chupasangre	140
Lipophrys trigloides	Caboz			118
Lithognathus mormyrus		Herrera		72
Macroramphosus scolopax	Trombeteiro	Trobeteiro	Trompetero	50
Manta birostris	Manta			18
Microchirus ocellatus			Soldado	132
Mobula mobular	Jamanta	Jamanta	Maroma	20
Mullus surmuletus	Salmonete	Salmonete	Salmonete	78
Muraena augusti	Moreia preta	Moreia preta	Morena	30
Muraena helena	Moreia pintada	Moreia pintada	Morena pintada	32
Mycteroperca fusca	Badejo	Badejo	Abade	56
Myliobatis aquila	Ratão-aguia		Peje águila	20
Myrichthys pardalis			Culebra	36
Oblada melanura	Dobrada		Galana	74
Oedalechilus labeo	Tainha	Tainha		52
Ophioblennius atlanticus	Velha	Roi anzois	Barriguda mora	120
Pagellus acarne	Besugo	Besugo	Besugo	72
Pagellus erythrinus	Bica		Breca	76
Pagrus pagrus	Pargo	Pargo	Bosinegro	74
Paraconger macrops	Congro de natura			40
Parapristipoma octolineatum			Burrito	82
Phycis phycis	Abrótea	Abrótea	Brota	44
Pomadasis incisus	Roncador		Roncador	80
Pomatomus saltator	Enchova	Anchova	Pejerrey	82
Priacanthus arenatus			Catalufa	64
Pseudocaranx dentex	Encharéu	Enchareu	Jurel	86
Pseudolepidaplois scrofa	Peixe cão	Peixe cão	Pejeperro	94
Raja clavata	Raia	Raia	Raya	26
Remora remora	Pegador	Meia sola	Pegador	110
Sarda sarda	Serralhao	Serra	Sierra	112
Sardinella aurita	Sardinha	Sardinha	Sardina	50
Sarpa salpa	Salema	Salema	Salema	70
Scorpaena maderensis	Rocaz	Rascasso	Rascacio	130
Scorpaena porcus		Rascasso	Rascacio	128
Scorpaena scrofa	Carneiro	Rocaz	Cantarero	128
Seriola dumerili	Charuteiro	Irio	Medregal	84
Seriola rivoliana	Charuteiro	Irio	Medregal	84

	MADEIRA	AZORES	CANARIES	p
Serranus atricauda	Garoupa	Garoupa	Cabrilla negra	60
Sparisoma cretense	Bodião	Veja	Vieja	106
Sphoeroides marmoratus	Sapinho	Sapo	Tamboril	138
Sphyraena viridensis	Bicuda	Bicuda	Bicuda	52
Spondyliosoma cantharus	Choupa		Chopa	68
Stephanolepis hispidus	Peixe porco galhudo		Gallo	134
Symphodus mediterraneus		Costureira		102
Syngnathus acus		Chicote	Pejepipa	48
Synodus saurus	Lagarto da costa	Peixe lagarto	Lagarto	28
Synodus synodus	Lagarto do rolo		Lagarto capitán	28
Taeniura grabata	Ratão		Chucho negro	22
Thalassoma pavo	Peixe verde	Rainha	Pejeverde	98
Thorogobius epphipiatus	Caboz de escama	Bochecha pintada	Caboso de las cuevas	124
Torpedo marmorata	Tremedeira		Tembladera	24
Trachinotus ovatus	Facaio	Prombeta	Palometa	88
Trachinus draco	Peixe aranha maior		Araña	108
Trachinus radiatus			Araña	108
Trachurus picturatus	Chicharro	Chicharro	Chicharro	88
Trigloporus lastoviza	Cabrinha		Rubio	126
Uranoscopus scaber	Papa tobaco		Pejesapo	110
Xyrichthys novacula	Peixe papagaio	Bodião da areia	Pejepeine	104
Zeus faber	Peixe galo	Peixe galo	Gallo de San Pedro	54

INDEX DEUTSCH

A

Achselfleckbrasse	72
Achtstreifengrunzer	82
Adlerrochen	20
Ährenfisch	46
Ährenfische	46
Ansauger	140
Atlantischer Großaugenbarsch	64
Atlantischer Lippfisch	104
Atlantischer Mönchsfisch	90
Augenfleck-Seezunge	132

B

Balearenaal	38
Bänderbrasse	68
Barrakudas	52
Bastardmakrele	88
Bermuda-Blaufisch	78
Beschuppte Blenniiden	122
Beutelbarsch	60
Blaubarsch	82
Blaubarsche	82
Blenniiden	116
Bonito	112
Brauner Blenni	118
Brauner Drachenkopf	128
Brauner Eidechsenfisch	28
Brauner Feilenfisch	134
Brauner Kugelfisch	138
Brauner Stechrochen	22
Brauner Zackenbarsch	58
Buckelkopfbrasse	78
Butte	130

D

Dicklippige Meeräsche	52
Dorsche	44
Dreiflosser	114
Drückerfische	134

E

Eberfisch	54
Eberfische	54
Echte Rochen	26
Eidechsenfische	28
Eingeweidefisch	142
Eingeweidefische	142

F

Feilenfische	134
Felsgrundel	124
Flossenloser Schlangenaal	36

G

Gabelmakrele	88
Gefleckte Hundszunge	132
Gefleckte Quappe	44
Gefleckter Lippfisch	100
Gefleckter Zitterrochen	24
Geißbrasse	66
Gelber Dreiflosser	114
Gelbflossen-Stachelmakrele	86
Gelbflossengrunzer	80
Gelbstriemen	70
Gestreifte Meerbarbe	78
Gestreifter Barrakuda	52
Gestreifter Knurrhahn	126
Gestreiftes Petermännchen	108
Glasauge	64
Goldgefleckter Schlangenaal	36
Goldstriemen	70
Grauer Blenni	118
Grauer Drückerfish	134
Großaugen	64
Großaugen-Meeraal	40
Große Bernsteinmakrele	84
Große Seenadel	48
Großer Gabeldorsch	44

Großer Roter Drachenkopf	128	Makaronesen-Zackenbarsch	56
Großes Petermännchen	108	Makrelen und Tune	112
Grundeln	124	Manta	18
Grüner Eidechsenfisch	28	Marmorbrasse	72
Grunzer	80	Marmorrochen	26
		Maskenmuräne	34
H		Meeraal	38
Halbschnäbler	42	Meeraale	38
Heringe	50	Meeräschen	52
Heringskönig	54	Meerbarben	78
Heringskönige	54	Meerbarbenkönig	62
Himmelsgucker	110	Meerbrassen	66
Himmelsgucker	110	Meerjunker	96
Hornhecht	42	Meerpfau	98
Hornhechte	42	Mittelmeer-Lippfisch	102
Hundszungen	132	Mittelmeer-Muräne	32
		Muränen	30
I			
Igelfisch	138	**N**	
Igelfische	138	Nagelrochen	26
		Neon-Riffbarsch	92
K			
Kardinalbarsche	62	**O**	
Kleine Bernsteinmakrele	84	Oblada	74
Kleiner Teufelsrochen	20	Ohrensardine	50
Knurrhähne	126		
Krokodilsmuräne	34	**P**	
Krötenfisch	144	Papageifisch	106
Krötenfische	144	Papageifische	106
Kuckuckslippfisch	100	Petermännchen	108
Kugelfische	136	Pilotbarsche	78
		Purpur-Ansauger	140
L			
Langschnäuziges Seepferdchen	48	**R**	
Leopardengrundel	124	Rauchflossenmakrele	86
Leopardenmuräne	34	Riffbarsche	90
Lippfische	94	Röhrenaal	40
		Rotbrasse	76
M		Roter Blenni	116
Madeira-Drachenkopf	130	Roter Fahnenbarsch	62

Roter Schweinsfisch	94	Zitterrochen	24
Rotlippenblenni	120	Zweibindenbrasse	66
		Zweifleck-Ansauger	140

S

Sackbrasse	74
Schermesserfisch	104
Schiffshalter	110
Schiffshalter	110
Schlangenaale	36
Schmetterlingsrochen	24
Schnepfenfisch	50
Schnepfenfische	50
Schopfblenni	122
Schriftbarsch	58
Schwarze Muräne	30
Schwarzer Stechrochen	22
Schwarzschwanz-Sägebarsch	60
Seenadeln	48
Seepferdchen	48
Seeschmetterling	120
Seezungen	132
Skorpionsfische	128
Spitzkopf-Kugelfisch	136
Spitzkopf-Zauberaal	36
Stachelmakrelen	84
Stechrochen	22
Streifenbrasse	68

T

Teufelsrochen	18
Tigermuräne	34
Trompetenfisch	46
Trompetenfische	46

W

Weitaugenbutt	130

Z

Zackenbarsche	56
Zauberaale	36

INDEX ENGLISCH

A
African striped grunt	82
Almaco jack	84
Amberjack	84
Atlantic bigeye	64
Atlantic bonito	112
Atlantic damselfish	90
Atlantic wrasse	104
Axillary bream	72
Axillary wrasse	102

B
Ballan wrasse	100
Barracudas	52
Bastard grunt	80
Bermuda sea chub	78
Bigeyes	64
Bigeye conger	40
Black bream	68
Black moray	30
Blacktail comber	60
Blennies	116
Blue runner	86
Bluefin damselfish	92
Bluefish	82
Bluefish	82
Boar fish	54
Boar fish	54
Bogue	70
Boxlip mullet	52
Breams	66
Brown blenny	118
Brown comber	60
Brown filefish	134
Brown lizardfish	28
Brown moray	34
Brown puffer	138
Brown scorpionfish	128

Butterfly blenny	120
Butterfly ray	24
Butterfly Rays	24

C
Cardinal Fish	62
Cardinal fish	62
Cleaver wrasse	104
Clingfish	140
Codfish	44
Comb grouper	56
Common bream	74
Common remora	110
Common stingray	22
Conger eel	38
Conger Eels	38
Cow bream	70
Cuckoo wrasse	100

D
Damselfish	90
Devil rays	18
Dories	54
Dusky grouper	58

E
Eagle ray	20
Eagle rays	20
Electic rays	24
Eyed sole	132

F
Fangtooth moray	34
Filefish	134
Finless snake eel	36
Frogfish	144
Frogfishes	144

G
Garden eel	40

Garfish	42
Glasseye	64
Goatfish	78
Gobies	124
Golden balearic conger	38
Golden-spotted snake eel	36
Gray Triggerfish	134
Great pipefish	48
Greater weever	108
Green lizardfish	28
Grey blenny	118
Groupers	56
Grunts	80
Guelly jack	86
Gurnards	126

H

Hairy blenny	122
Halfbeak	42
Halfbeaks	42
Herrings	50
Horse mackerel	88

J

Jacks	84
John dory	54

L

Larger forkbeard	44
Left-eye Flounders	130
Leopard-spotted goby	124
Lizardfish	28
Lump-headed bream	78

M

Mackerels and Tunas	112
Madeira scorpionfish	130
Manta ray	18
Marbled electic ray	24
Mediterranean moray	32

Moray Eels	30
Mullets	52

N

Needlefish	42

P

Painted comber	58
Pandora	76
Parrotfish	106
Parrotfish	106
Pearlfish	142
Pipefish	48
Pompano	88
Porcupinefish	138
Pufferfish	136
Purple clingfish	140

R

Rainbow wrasse	96
Red blenny	116
Red hogfish	94
Red scorpionfish	128
Redlip blenny	120
Rock goby	124
Round sardinella	50
Round stingray	22

S

Saddled bream	74
Sand smelt	46
Sand Smelts	46
Scaled Blennies	122
Scorpionfish	128
Sea Chubs	78
Seahorse	48
Seahorses	48
Sharksuckers	110
Sharpnose puffer	136
Sharpnose sorcerer eel	36

Skates	26	**Y**	
Small devil ray	20	Yellow triplefin	114
Snake Eels	36		
Snipe Fish	50	**Z**	
Snipe fish	50	Zebra bream	68
Soles	132		
Sorcerer Eels	36		
Spotted rockling	44		
Spotted tonguesole	132		
Stargazer	110		
Stargazers	110		
Stingrays	22		
Streaked gurnard	126		
Streaked weever	108		
Striped barracudas	52		
Striped bream	72		
Striped mullet	78		
Swallowtail seaperch	62		

T

Thornback ray	26
Tonguesoles	132
Triggerfish	134
Triplefin blennies	114
Trumpetfish	46
Trumpetfish	46
Turkish wrasse	98
Two-banded bream	66
Twospot clingfish	140

U

Undulate ray	26

W

Weevers	108
White bream	66
Wide-eyed flounder	130
Wrasses	94

INDEX LATEIN

A

Abudefduf luridus	92
Antennariidae	144
Antennarius nummifer	144
Anthias anthias	62
Apogon imberbis	62
Apogonidae	62
Apterichthus caecus	36
Ariosoma balearicum	38
Atherina presbyter	46
Atherinidae	46
Aulostomidae	46
Aulostomus strigosus	46

B

Balistes carolinensis	134
Balistidae	134
Belone belone	42
Belonidae	42
Blenniidae	116
Blennius ocellaris	120
Boops boops	70
Bothidae	130
Bothus podas	130

C

Canthigaster rostrata	136
Caproidae	54
Capros aper	54
Carangidae	84
Caranx crysos	86
Carapidae	142
Carapus acus	142
Centrolabrus trutta	104
Chromis limbata	90
Clupeidae	50
Conger conger	38
Congridae	38
Coris julis	96
Cynoglossidae	132

D

Dasyatidae	22
Dasyatis pastinaca	22
Dentex gibbosus	78
Diodon hystrix	138
Diodontidae	138
Diplecogaster bimaculata	140
Diplodus cervinus	68
Diplodus sargus	66
Diplodus vulgaris	66

E

Echeneididae	110
Enchelycore anatina	34
Epinephelus marginatus	58

F

Faciolella oxyrhyncha	36

G

Gadidae	44
Gaidropsarus guttatus	44
Gobius paganellus	124
Gobiesocidae	140
Gobiidae	124
Gymnothorax unicolor	34
Gymnura altavela	24
Gymnuridae	24

H

Haemulidae	80
Hemirhamphidae	42
Hemirhamphus balao	42
Heteroconger longissimus	40
Heteropriacanthus cruentatus	64
Hippocampus ramulosus	48

K
Kyphosidae	78
Kyphosus sectatrix	78

L
Labridae	94
Labrisomidae	122
Labrisomus nuchipinnis	122
Labrus bergylta	100
Labrus bimaculatus	100
Lepadogaster candollei	140
Lipophrys trigloides	118
Lithognathus mormyrus	72

M
Macroramphosidae	50
Macroramphosus scolopax	50
Manta birostris	18
Microchirus ocellatus	132
Mobula mobular	20
Mobulidae	18
Monacanthidae	134
Mugilidae	52
Mullidae	78
Mullus surmuletus	78
Muraena augusti	30
Muraena helena	32
Muraenidae	30
Mycteroperca fusca	56
Myliobatidae	20
Myliobatis aquila	20
Myrichthys pardalis	36

N
Nettastomidae	36

O
Oblada melanura	74
Oedalechilus labeo	52
Ophichthidae	36
Ophioblennius atlanticus	120

P
Pagellus acarne	72
Pagellus erythrinus	76
Pagrus pagrus	74
Parablennius incognitus	118
Parablennius ruber	116
Paraconger macrops	40
Parapristipoma octolineatum	82
Phycis phycis	44
Pomacentridae	90
Pomadasis incisus	80
Pomatomidae	82
Pomatomus saltator	82
Priacanthidae	64
Priacanthus arenatus	64
Pseudocaranx dentex	86
Pseudolepidaplois scrofa	94

R
Raja clavata	26
Raja undulata	26
Rajidae	26
Remora remora	110

S
Sarda sarda	112
Sardinella aurita	50
Sarpa salpa	70
Scaridae	106
Scombridae	112
Scorpaena maderensis	130
Scorpaena porcus	128
Scorpaena scrofa	128
Scorpaenidae	128
Seriola dumerili	84
Seriola rivoliana	84
Serranidae	56
Serranus atricauda	60
Serranus hepatus	60
Serranus scriba	58
Soleidae	132

Sparidae	66
Sparisoma cretense	106
Sphoeroides marmoratus	138
Sphyraena viridensis	52
Sphyraenidae	52
Spondyliosoma cantharus	68
Stephanolepis hispidus	134
Symphodus mediterraneus	102
Symphurus reticulatus	132
Syngnathidae	48
Syngnathus acus	48
Synodontidae	28
Synodus saurus	28
Synodus synodus	28

T

Taeniura grabata	22
Tetraodontidae	136
Thalassoma pavo	98
Thorogobius epphipiatus	124
Torpedinidae	24
Torpedo marmorata	24
Trachinidae	108
Trachinotus ovatus	88
Trachinus draco	108
Trachinus radiatus	108
Trachurus picturatus	88
Triglidae	126
Trigloporus lastoviza	126
Tripterygiidae	114
Tripterygion delaisi	114

U

Uranoscopidae	110
Uranoscopus scaber	110

X

Xyrichthys novacula	104

Z

Zeidae	54
Zeus faber	54

Bildnachweis - Photo Credit

(o = oben/above, u = unten/below, i = insert, l = links/left, r = rechts/ right)
Otmar von Alst: 25o, u, 39u, 41o, 43o, 47o, u, 53u, 59u, 63u, 69u, 75o, u, 79o, 97o, 101u, 105o, u, 127o. **Jorge de Castro**: 35o, 69o. **Helmut Corneli**: 27u, 55u, 60u. **Walter Kleinen** 83o, 123. **Joe Klenk**: 47oi, 49. **Andreas Koffka**: 21u, 23, 35u, 59o, 65o, 81, 109o, 111o, 133o. **Theo Mühlenberg**: 135o. **Peter Nahke**: 17u, 29u, 73u, 79u, 97u, 104u, 109u, 121o, 135u, 139u. **Bernd Reckmeyer**: 17o, 107ui, 137o, 137ur, 139o. **Peter Wirtz**: alle anderen/ all others.

LITERATURVERZEICHNIS - BIBLIOGRAPHY

Bauchot, M.L. & Pras, A. : Guide des poissons marins d'Europe. Paris 1980
Blache, J. & Cadenat, J. & Stauch, A. : Clés de determination des poissons de mer signalés dans l'Atlantique oriental (entre le 20^0 Parallele N. et le 15^0 Parallele S.). Faune Tropicale XVIII, O.R.S.T.O.M., Paris 1970.
Brito, A. : Catálogo de los peces de las Canarias. F. Lemmus, La Laguna, Tenerife 1991
Fischer, W., Bianchi, G., Scott, W. B. : FAO species identification sheets for fishery purposes: Eastern central Atlantic. Rom 1981
Lythgoe, J. & G.: Fishes of the Sea. Blanford Press, London 1991^2
Maul, G. E. : Lista sistematica dos peixes da Madeira. In: Vertebrados da Madeira, Vol 2, 137-181, 1949.
Quéro, J. C. et al. : Checklist of the fishes of the Eastern tropical Atlantic. UNESCO, Paris 1990, 2 vols.
Randall, John: Caribbean Reef Fishes. T.F.H., Neptune City 1983^2
Robins, C. R. et al.: A field guide to Atlantic Coast Fishes. Houghton Mifflin Comp., Boston 1986
Whitehead, P.J.P. et al. : Fishes of the North-eastern Atlantic and the Mediterranean. Unesco, Paris 1984, 3 vols.
Wirtz, P. & Nahke, P.: Unterwasserführer Karibik Fische * Underwater Guide Caribbean Fishes. Naglschmid, Stuttgart 1993

DANKSAGUNG - ACKNOWLEDGEMENT

Ein Teil der Fotos in diesem Buch wurde während eines 6-monatigen Forschungsaufenthaltes am Departamento de Oceanografia e Pescas der Universität der Azoren gemacht. Ich danke der Secretaria Regional da Agricultura e Pescas der autonomen Region der Azoren für die Finanzierung und Ricardo Serrao Santos für die Einladung, an das Institut zu kommen. Die Fotos bei Madeira wurden von den Tauchbasen von Joe Klenk und Rainer Waschkewitz gemacht, die mich über viele Jahre freundlich aufgenommen haben und von denen ich viel gelernt habe. Mein Freund Peter Nahke half mir bei der Bildauswahl.

Dr. Peter Wirtz ist Meeresbiologe und Verhaltensforscher. Bei vielen Reisen zu Atlantischen Inseln und den Atlantischen Küsten Afrikas hat er noch unbekannte Fische entdeckt und als erster beschrieben. Seit 1992 hat er den Lehrstuhl für Meeresbiologie an der Universität von Madeira/Portugal. Zusammen mit Dr. Peter Nahke hat er bereits die Bände über die Fische der Malediven und die Fische der Karibik in der Serie "Unterwasserführer" verfaßt.

UNTERWASSERFÜHRER - UNDERWATER GUIDES

Unterwasserführer Rotes Meer: Fische / Underwater Guide Red Sea: Fish, Helmut Debelius, 168 Seiten, 2. Auflage 1990, ISBN 3-925342-18-4

Unterwasserführer Rotes Meer: Niedere Tiere / Under Water Guide Red Sea: Invertebrates, Peter Schmid und Dietmar Paschke, 168 Seiten, 2. Auflage 1990, ISBN 3-925342-10-9

Unterwasserführer Malediven: Fische / Underwater Guide Maldives: Fish, Peter Nahke und Peter Wirtz, 168 Seiten, 2. Auflage 1992, ISBN 3-925342-59-1

Unterwasserführer Karibik: Fische / Underwater Guide The Carribean: Fish, Peter Wirtz und Peter Nahke, 176 Seiten, 1993, ISBN 3-927913-26-X

Unterwasserführer Europäische Binnengewässer, Bernd Humberg, 200 Seiten, 1994, ISBN 3-927913-44-8

TAUCHREISEFÜHRER

Tauchreiseführer Malta, Arnd Rödiger, 80 Seiten, 1990, ISBN 3-925342-48-6

Tauchreiseführer Kärnten, Herbert Frei, 128 Seiten, 1994, ISBN 3-925342-94-X

Tauchreiseführer Bonaire, Michael Jung, 152 Seiten, 1992, ISBN 3-927913-12-X

Tauchreiseführer Sinai, Peter Schmidt und Claudia Kreutzer-Schmid, 128 Seiten, ISBN 3-925342-99-0

Tauchreiseführer Die Inseln von Hyères, Margot und Franz Ebersoldt, 128 Seiten, 1987, ISBN 3-925342-43-5

Tauchreiseführer Costa Brava, Dietmar Paschke, 120 Seiten, 1989, ISBN 3-925342-54-0

Tauchreiseführer Korsika, Franz Brümmer und Werner Baumeister, 104 Seiten, 1992, ISBN 3-925342-19-2

VERLAG STEPHANIE NAGLSCHMID
Rotebühlstr. 87A, 70178 Stuttgart, Telefon 0711/626878, Fax 0711/612323